PRAISE FOR
Help Anxious Kids in a Stressful World

"This book arrives at a time of significant societal stress and offers insight and relief. It is informative, practical, and, most importantly, oriented toward taking immediate action to relieve anxiety in our children. It is rare to encounter a publication so informative and solution based that teachers and counselors at every level can use to enhance their students' lives. No child is immune from anxiety. Having worked as a professional counselor and therapist at all levels of the educational system for over thirty years, I recognize the need our school staff has for solution-based literature related to anxiety. In addition, as a private practitioner having specialized working as a family therapist, it is apparent to me that *Help Anxious Kids in a Stressful World* would be a welcome addition to any therapist's or counselor's library."—**Jack Gilbert, M.A.,** bilingual licensed professional and marriage-family counselor, former school psychologist

---

"*Help Anxious Kids in a Stressful World* is a timely and much-needed resource. As an educator consulting with school leaders across the country, I know the issue of childhood anxiety is real. It enormously impacts the challenges teachers face as they work with their students. Principals are searching for strategies to help teachers and their students." —**Eileen M. Reed, Ed.D.,** ESR Consulting

---

"Anxiety rates in children are on the rise, and our children need us to notice when they're struggling and to help them when they don't have the ability to ask for help themselves. I love that this book provides actionable, practical knowledge so that, regardless of experience, prior knowledge, and background, teachers and others involved with students can help make a real difference." —**Alison Bogle,** parenting blogger, writer, and speaker

---

"A much-needed resource for teachers on student anxiety. Preventing and relieving anxiety is essential to student well-being, and without intervention, anxiety can become an obstacle to students' success in school and in life. This book is focused on supporting and caring for children and youth and will be a wonderful resource for teachers and educational leaders as well as parents and other community members." —**Gloria T. Alter, M.A., Ed.D.,** counselor, teacher educator, and author of *The Human Rights Imperative in Teacher Education*

"As a school principal serving students who suffer from anxiety and other forms of trauma, this book has been a godsend. It's a tremendous help to myself as a leader and to my staff, who are constantly searching for valuable tools to support our highest-need students. Children are our most valuable asset to the survival of our communities and deserve the best support they can get through our public education system. The tools provided in *Help Anxious Kids in a Stressful World* are practical and immediately applicable to any classroom." —**Amy E. Garza, M.Ed.,** principal of Medio Creek Elementary School, SWISD, San Antonio, Texas

25 Classroom Strategies

Help Anxious Kids in a Stressful World

David Campos, Ph.D. ■ Kathleen McConnell Fad, Ph.D.

free spirit
PUBLISHING®

Library of Congress Cataloging-in-Publication Data

Names: Campos, David, author. | McConnell, Kathleen, author.
Title: Help anxious kids in a stressful world : 25 classroom strategies /
 David Campos, Kathleen McConnell Fad.
Description: Minneapolis, MN : Free Spirit Publishing, an imprint of Teacher
 Created Materials, [2024] | Includes bibliographical references and index.
 | Audience: Ages 4-18 (provided by Free Spirit Publishing, an imprint of
 Teacher Created Materials, Inc.)
Identifiers: LCCN 2023008861 (print) | LCCN 2023008860 (ebook) | ISBN
 9798885543262 (paperback) | ISBN 9798885543279 (ebook) | ISBN
 9798885543286 (epub) | ISBN 9798885543286_q(epub) | ISBN
 9798885543279_q(ebook) | ISBN 9798885543262_q(paperback)
Subjects: LCSH: Anxiety in children--Juvenile literature. | Child
 psychology--Juvenile literature. | School psychology--Juvenile literature.
 | BISAC: EDUCATION / Teaching / Methods & Strategies | EDUCATION / Special
 Education / Behavioral, Emotional & Social Disabilities
Classification: LCC BF723.A5 C36 2024 (ebook) | LCC BF723.A5 (print) | DDC
 155.4/1246 23/eng/20230--dc17
LC record available at https://lccn.loc.gov/2023008861

Free Spirit Publishing does not have control over or assume responsibility for author or third-party websites and their content. At the time of this book's publication, all facts and figures cited within are the most current available. All telephone numbers, addresses, and website URLs are accurate and active; all publications, organizations, websites, and other resources exist as described in this book; and all have been verified as of March 2023. If you find an error or believe that a resource listed here is not as described, please contact Free Spirit Publishing.

Edited by Christine Zuchora-Walske
Cover and interior design by Colleen Pidel

Printed in China

Free Spirit Publishing
An imprint of Teacher Created Materials
9850 51st Avenue North, Suite 100
Minneapolis, MN 55442
(612) 338-2068
help4kids@freespirit.com
freespirit.com

FSC
www.fsc.org
MIX
Paper | Supporting
responsible forestry
FSC® C144853

Dedication

We would like to dedicate this book to our family and friends, whose love and support enrich our lives and give us confidence to pursue projects that help school communities nationwide. This book also honors teachers everywhere, who work hard to help students achieve academic excellence and social and emotional well-being.

Acknowledgments

We would like to express our deepest gratitude to the Free Spirit Publishing team, especially Tom Rademacher, who helped us clarify our ideas, and Christine Zuchora-Walske, for her editorial expertise. Finally, this book would not be possible if it were not for our longtime friendship and collaboration. Our collegial support for one another is an ongoing source of joy and inspiration.

Contents

Anxiety in Children Is Real and Widespread

You likely selected this book because something about your students is concerning you. Perhaps your students seem uneasy, worried, or nervous. These anxiety-related symptoms are on the rise, especially since the COVID-19 pandemic began. There is a good chance that students are not performing like previous cohorts because they are experiencing anxiety like never before. To complicate matters, they might not have an anxiety diagnosis nor receive services but they still need your help. To help you help your students, in this book we discuss childhood anxiety, why it is increasing, and what you can do to offer support, guidance, and strategies to prevent and moderate anxiety's effects on students.

We are strongly committed to ensuring that teachers, regardless of their prior knowledge and backgrounds, have a wide range of easy-to-understand, practical, useful instructional tools for working with anxious students. Whether you are a new or experienced teacher, whether you're in general or special education, this book is for you. You can learn about the characteristics of anxiety, its physiological origins, and the domains of student learning it impacts. Most importantly, you will learn what to do and how to do it. The strategies in this book are supported by research, easy to implement, and designed specifically for teachers. We know that if you use them, they will help your students with anxiety.

Why We Wrote This Book

We are former classroom teachers—in both general and special education—with more than sixty combined years of experience working with children who have special needs, as well as with their teachers and school leadership teams to improve lesson design and delivery, learning environments, and collaboration. Our classroom experiences taught us that many children, especially those identified with disabilities, are on the social margins at school, and that position often leads to loneliness. When we explored this topic more deeply, our research confirmed that childhood loneliness is far more common than we originally guessed. To address this issue, we wrote a book on childhood loneliness titled *Lonely Kids in a Connected World: What Teachers Can Do* (2021).

As we designed our intervention strategies for *Lonely Kids in a Connected World*, we combed through hundreds of scientific articles, which showed that many aspects of loneliness are intertwined with childhood anxiety. (You'll find a comprehensive definition of childhood anxiety in chapter 1, but for now you can think of anxiety as an uncomfortable feeling caused by fears and worries.) The next thing we knew, we were exploring childhood anxiety too. We knew that anxiety is a significant challenge for some students; after all, we taught children with special needs, and many of them were medically diagnosed with anxiety disorders and/or emotional behavior disorders. But our focus at the time of this exploration was on students who have recurring heightened stress (anxiety) and are *not* identified as having a disorder as defined by the Individuals with Disabilities Education Act (IDEA).

In the children's mental health field, there are two diagnostic frameworks: educational and medical. In education, students with anxiety are referred to as having an emotional behavior disorder according to the criteria of IDEA. Medical professionals use the *Diagnostic and Statistical Manual of Mental Disorders, Fifth Edition (DSM-5)*, to diagnose specific mental health conditions, including several types of anxiety. While some students may be diagnosed both educationally and medically, not all students are. The students who quality for an emotional behavior disorder diagnosis under IDEA or Section 504 of the Rehabilitation Act of 1973 have either individualized education programs (IEPs) or 504 plans, which address their needs, including those related to an anxiety disorder. Many anxious students have no diagnosis in either framework. We believe strongly in supporting these students as well, for two reasons: (1) early intervention may prevent the need for an anxiety diagnosis; and (2) some students need help coping with problematic behaviors that are interfering with their learning. In short: these students need help *now*.

Our review of the research revealed how highly prevalent anxiety is in children and adolescents. One in five children have anxiety (Racine, McArthur, and Cooke 2021). So, in a classroom of twenty-five students, five may be overwhelmed with fear, worry, or unease enough to interfere with school activities. Students who are anxious have a difficult time learning and socializing with others. Their brains simply do not allow them to function effectively in the classroom.

Changing Attitudes Toward Anxiety

Only recently have mental health experts considered childhood anxiety a serious problem. A 2016 *Science News* article on childhood anxiety compared the current scientific view to that of decades earlier. In 1966, the editors of the journal wrote: "A most important finding [in a recent study] was that the fearful or anxious children, defined . . . as those with seven or more worries, did not seem to be in any particular psychological trouble. . . . Anxieties may be part of normal child development." Fifty years later, the *Science News* editors clarified: "Actually, there *is* reason to worry about anxious children. Kids with anxiety disorders, depression or behavioral problems are especially likely to develop a range of difficulties as young adults, say researchers who conducted a long-term study published in 2015. The same goes for kids whose anxiety, mood or behavior issues cause daily problems but don't qualify as psychiatric ailments" (Bower 2016).

Anxiety and fear were once considered a common aspect of development that children outgrew (Burke 2007). Many children today, however, have circumstances in their lives that cause them recurring and overwhelming distress, which can adversely affect their learning (American Psychiatric Association 2013). Isolated events such as single acts of sexual abuse and regular maltreatment from harsh rearing practices such as parental physical abuse as discipline, threatening environmental conditions such as neighborhood violence, and other home-life stressors such as financial or food insecurity can cause children undue anxiety (National Scientific Council on the Developing Child 2010).

The Impact of COVID-19

We conducted much of our research well before the COVID-19 pandemic began. Even before the pandemic, anxiety disorders were consistently the most prevalent mental health disorder of children and adolescents in the United States. From 2008 to 2018, there was a 17 percent increase in the number of anxiety disorders (Child Mind Institute 2018).

Anxiety is even more pervasive now because of COVID. In a study that surveyed seventy-five thousand high school students across the United States between fall 2018 and fall 2020, 56 percent of participants reported that their stress about school had increased during the pandemic (Challenge Success 2021). This study found that girls and students of color reported especially high levels of stress (68 percent and 63 percent, respectively)—both higher than their male and White counterparts, 48 and 55 percent of whom, respectively, reported high levels of stress. The majority of students in the study were having a difficult time engaging in their learning, and they experienced strained relationships at school.

Nearly a year after the Challenge Success report, the *New York Times* published an article describing similar effects of the pandemic. The children and adolescents interviewed for this piece shared anxious sentiments like the following (Fortin and Heyward 2022):

- "Anxiety is all around me."
- "I am deeply anxious about spreading the disease to family and friends."
- "I feel unstable and cautious at school."
- "I have bouts of loneliness."
- "It feels like the pandemic is never going to end."
- "What if things get taken away from me?"
- "I miss my friends."
- "I am withdrawn."
- "I feel disconnected."

These articles made us wonder: how would children we know describe anxiety in their current lives? We asked two young students, a fourth grader and a second grader, about their feelings related to COVID and anxiety. Their responses echoed the feelings reported in the *New York Times* article.

One student wrote, "I feel stressed out and I feel like there's a knot in my stomach." Later, when we asked about the impact of COVID, she explained, "I have felt a little more anxious because we have had to wear masks in school because of COVID-19."

I feel stressed out and I feel like theres a knot in my stomach.

The second student described what anxiety in school feels like to her. She wrote, "Being anxious makes me feel behind. It also makes me feel angry." COVID-19 had a direct impact on her anxiety. She explained, "The pandemic has made me feel more anxious because I get sick often."

I have felt a little more anxious because we have had to wear masks in school because of covid 19.

A recent meta-analysis found an increase in the global prevalence rates of both depression and anxiety. The research revealed that the "prevalence estimates of clinically elevated child and adolescent depression and anxiety were 25.2% and 20.5%, respectively. The prevalence of depression and anxiety symptoms during COVID-19 have doubled compared with prepandemic estimates" (Racine, McArthur, and Cooke 2021). We attribute the dramatic increase in anxiety disorders among children and adolescents to many factors. These include isolation due to school closures, increased stress on families, and fewer social interactions with peers.

The authors of the meta-analysis point out that demand for mental health services will likely increase, as will the need to allocate resources to serve young people with anxiety, depression, and related disorders. They note that 80 percent of children rely on school-based services to meet their mental health needs, and school closures rendered these services unavailable to many school-age children and adolescents. They make a case for improving the delivery of behavioral health support and treatment to young people and guiding them and their families to keep consistent, predictable routines for screen use, sleep, and physical activity.

Given all the evidence showing that the pandemic has had a serious negative impact on children and adolescents, we were encouraged when US Surgeon General Vivek Murthy issued an advisory calling for a swift and coordinated response to the "real" and "widespread" mental health crisis among children and adolescents.

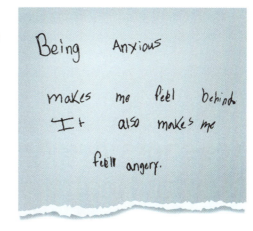

"The COVID-19 pandemic dramatically altered young people's experiences at home, at school, and in the community," he explained, "and the effect these challenges have had on their mental health is devastating" (Office of the Surgeon General 2021). The advisory calls on all Americans to work together to support the nation's children during this crisis. His recommendations include the following priorities:

1. Recognize that mental health is an essential part of overall health.

2. Empower youth and their families to recognize, manage, and learn from difficult emotions.

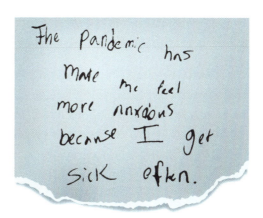

3. Ensure that every child has access to high-quality, affordable, and culturally competent mental health care.

4. Support the mental health of children and youth in educational, community, and childcare settings.

The aims of this book align with Murthy's recommendations. We want to empower young people to recognize, manage, and learn from challenging feelings with the help of their teachers. Many children and adolescents with anxiety express their difficult feelings by way of stress-related behaviors, such as:

- excessive crying or irritation
- returning to outgrown behaviors
- excessive worry or sadness
- unhealthy sleeping or eating
- difficulty paying attention and concentrating
- unexplained headaches or body pain
- using alcohol, tobacco, or other drugs

These behaviors—if persistent and untreated—can become ingrained. We hope we can alleviate some of these behaviors and prevent future difficulties by giving teachers many tools—our action strategies—to help students regulate their emotions, cope with their anxiety, and establish friendly relationships with their peers. We are committed to making it as easy as possible for educators to teach their students social and emotional skills related to anxiety.

Teachers Are Key to Students' Mental Health

We understand that many teachers do not consider themselves mental health experts, that their primary role is to educate children and adolescents, and that they have numerous demands piled high on their plate of responsibilities at school. In addition, teachers may lack professional training for helping students with anxiety. But teachers are critical to children's emotional well-being. Not only the COVID pandemic, but also enticing and addictive digital technologies, the constant presence of social media, and other social changes contribute to unprecedented stress on children (Pew Research Center 2015). The teacher's role has expanded in response, to encompass identifying students' mental health symptoms and helping reduce their anxiety (Ginsburg et al. 2019).

The good news is that when teachers are trained in and teach social and emotional curricula (for example, problem-solving, coping, and relationship skills), the effects on student outcomes are overwhelmingly positive. Equipped with resources such as this book, teachers can strengthen children's abilities to deal with anxious behaviors that lead to difficulties in the classroom. Research evidence shows that teachers are quite capable of applying anxiety-reducing strategies (Ginsburg et al. 2019). Additionally, teachers can create emotionally supportive settings promoting social interactions in the classroom that encourage friendships, teamwork, and collaboration, especially in a period of development when peers play a substantial role in children's everyday lives (Ybañez-Llorente 2014). Significant research shows that school-based interventions to treat anxiety can have lasting effects on students' emotional, behavioral, and educational functioning (Weir 2017).

Teachers are ideally positioned to carry out prevention and intervention strategies that target anxiety for several reasons:

- **Teachers see students daily.** So, they can recognize when children have anxiety and need intervention (Ybañez-Llorente 2014). Classroom social dynamics often trigger anxiety in students more than in other environments, such as home or church, where children may be more comfortable because they get individual support and frequent reassurances (Herzig-Anderson et al. 2012). Some children may be overly sensitive about performing in front of others, for example, or they may stress over how their peers may negatively evaluate or behave toward them, such as by rejecting or excluding them from social circles (Ybañez-Llorente 2014).

Teachers can also help students identify when anxiety emerges and manage it effectively (Ginsburg et al. 2019). Through daily interactions, teachers can continuously monitor how well their students are applying learned intervention skills (McLoone, Hudson, and Rapee 2006).

- **In the classroom, students are already in a setting designed for learning.** So, why not teach them life skills to cope with challenges and negative emotions that could otherwise plague them for years? Classrooms offer perfect opportunities for social skills practice in real-life, everyday situations. Through class- and team-building exercises, students can receive authentic feedback and support from their peers that can lead to a climate of trust and caring.

- **Schools are accessible and convenient for caregivers.** When children receive anxiety-related support and instruction at school, their families don't have to worry about taking time off from work or about transporting their child to a clinic. Moreover, they do not need to incur costs or deal with medical referrals or waiting lists. Research shows that therapy provided to children outside of school is often not enough (Hugh-Jones et al. 2020). School-based intervention can enhance whatever therapy children receive on their personal time. Schoolwide prevention and intervention programs also have the potential to normalize mental health care (Killu and Crundwell 2016). Teachers can help destigmatize mental health conditions when they teach coping strategies with a positive attitude (Herzig-Anderson et al. 2012; McLoone, Hudson, and Rapee 2006). When children learn the benefits of good mental health habits and coping strategies, they begin to recognize the importance of improving and maintaining well-being.

- **The earlier intervention is provided, the less severe the impact of anxiety will be.** "Anxious behaviors are less entrenched in younger children and thus may be easier to modify" (Donovan and March 2014). Teachers can impart skills early on—in elementary school, for example—rather than waiting until the child is an adolescent or young adult, when anxiety might be more challenging to treat. Teaching students how to handle negative emotions early in life can reduce the chances of anxiety developing into psychopathological disorder (Caldwell et al. 2019).

How Anxiety Might Look in School

Teachers, counselors, administrators, and other educators likely encounter students with anxiety in school every day. Let's look at three students who, their teachers believe, suffer from anxiety. As you reflect on each student's behavior, think about these questions:

- What are your first impressions of the student's behavior?

- How might anxiety contribute to the student's behavior?

- How does the student's anxiety inhibit their learning?

Marc is a sixth grader who is quiet and compliant. He does not like to work in pairs or groups and is often seen alone in the hallways, in the cafeteria, and outside after lunch. In class, when his peers tease or make fun of him, he withdraws and seems to be on the verge of tears. Teachers have noted that he complains of stomachaches and is regularly red-faced.

Fourth grader **Rosa** is meticulous when she does class- and homework. She is careful about how she positions each letter of her handwriting and works attentively so that her assignments have no smudges or tears. Any work that requires a drawing is precisely crafted. Rosa has meltdowns when she doesn't have time to finish her classwork or when her assignments do not meet her standard of excellence. She eats very little at lunch because she doesn't like when her peers watch her eat. Both her teacher and her mother call Rosa a perfectionist.

Third grader **Miguel** is new to his school after having moved three times this school year. After he is dropped off at school, he walks into the building slowly, dragging his backpack behind him. He does not smile when he is greeted by school administrators, nor does he answer their questions about his breakfast. He stands quietly in the hallway, even though all students are supposed to wait in the cafeteria. His behavior seems oppositional, but his teacher senses that he is afraid and lonely in the new school. At times, he refuses to follow even simple directions and has escalated to throwing his backpack and running out of the room.

There is no single profile of a student with anxiety, as these examples show. Children are unique, and their anxiety can present differently depending on their age, experiences, and numerous other factors. These and other issues will be explored throughout the book.

About This Book

We've organized this book into two parts. Part 1 establishes a framework for understanding anxiety, its causes, and different ways it can present in young people. Part 2 offers twenty-five practical action strategies, including an introductory chapter explaining how to use them and a matrix to identify which strategies may be most useful for specific situations.

Part 1: Understanding Anxiety

Chapter 1: Childhood Anxiety: Background and Definitions

First, we explain the population of students we hope to serve through our action strategies. It includes two key groups: (1) children who have anxiety that interferes with their academic achievement and social relationships but are not identified with a disorder or receiving related services, and (2) children whose anxiety is a diagnosed mental disorder and who have an IEP or a 504 plan and receive accommodations and/or related services. We distinguish anxiety that's a normal human experience from anxiety that interferes with learning and socialization. We finish with a description of the most common anxiety disorders.

Chapter 2: A Framework for Childhood Anxiety: Prevalence, Characteristics, and Features

This chapter shows how pervasive anxiety is and describes its immediate and long-term effects when left untreated. We also discuss how teachers can expect anxiety to look in children in four domains:

- physiological
- behavioral
- social and emotional
- academic or cognitive

These domains serve as the foundation for our action strategies. We conclude by explaining how anxiety can contribute to academic and social downward spirals.

Chapter 3: Causes of Childhood Anxiety and Biological Stress Responses: The Brains of Anxious Children

Here we discuss two broad but critical facets of anxiety: (1) its causes and (2) how children's brains respond when they experience anxiety. Understanding the biological nature of anxiety is useful when teachers present strategies to help children regulate their stress responses. Since we are not neurologists, in this chapter we offer a simplified description of the brain's system and structure.

Chapter 4: Addressing Childhood Anxiety in School: School-Based Interventions, Programs, and Social and Emotional Learning

This chapter explains the importance of prevention and intervention programs at school and how cognitive behavioral therapy (CBT) successfully treats children who suffer from anxiety. We also provide key background on social and emotional learning (SEL), which teaches children long-term skills to use when they experience stressful life events.

Part 2: Twenty-Five Action Strategies to Prevent and Reduce Anxiety

Chapter 5: Action Strategies Explained

In this chapter, you'll learn about the components of the action strategies, the ready-set-go three-step method, and the four domains, or general categories, associated with the childhood anxiety: physiological, behavioral, social and emotional, and academic or cognitive. A table helps select strategies to use based on your observations. The chapter closes with how to start using the action strategies, with advice that includes considerations before, during, and after instruction.

The Strategies

These twenty-five research-based strategies support students with anxiety-related behaviors. Each strategy includes the domains that the intervention addresses, the recommended instructional arrangements, and whether it uses a cognitive behavioral therapy (CBT) component. Each strategy has a simple ready-set-go format that eliminates the need for the teacher to write a complicated lesson plan. The Ready step answers the fundamental question *Why is this strategy important?* The Set step prepares you to teach the strategy. The Go step outlines procedures, materials, and activity sheets to use.

Special Features

In each chapter, we provide these special features to help you absorb what you're learning and think through your own situation:

- **Think About It** provides questions for readers to reflect on as they read upcoming sections.

- **Classroom Connection** offers ideas for immediate classroom implementation.

- **In the Research** presents research information that makes sense to just about everyone.

- **Here's What. So What? Now What?** appears at the end of each chapter. It asks questions to help you review what you've learned in that chapter. In the table of contents, a pencil icon denotes this teacher reflection form.

- **Student activity sheets** accompany most of the strategies to help you implement them. In the table of contents, pencil icons also denote student activity sheets.

How to Use This Book

If you are reading this book, you are likely seeking ideas for students whom you believe have—or who are diagnosed with—anxiety. Depending on your knowledge about childhood anxiety, you can read and benefit from this book in a variety of ways. Unlike most textbooks for teachers, this book needn't be read in order from the first to the last page.

If you know nothing about childhood anxiety, start with chapter 1. If you know a little about childhood anxiety, but you want to know the latest definition, information, and prevalence, then chapters 1 and 2 are your starting points. If you have special interest in the biology of anxiety, chapter 3 has some great information. If you know all of that, and want to know more about school-based interventions and social and emotional learning, start with chapter 4. Teachers will find this chapter especially relevant. If you are well educated about anxiety and you are a teacher ready to implement strategies to support your anxious students, part 2 is for you. All the tools you need, including engaging activity sheets, a simple three-step model for implementation, and a user-friendly format make this section a valuable resource. Just when you feel that you've tried everything and nothing works, this section will help you and your students succeed and feel good about what you're doing.

We know how difficult it can be to teach students who exhibit anxiety-related behaviors, especially when the available tools, resources, and information seem too complicated to use in the classroom. We are confident that when you use our practical strategies, they will have a positive effect on your students' lives and yours. We'll be thinking of you.

David Campos

Kathy McConnell Fad

Part 1: Understanding
Anxiety

CHAPTER 1

Childhood Anxiety:
Background and Definitions

Childhood anxiety is real and widespread, and the COVID-19 pandemic has increased childhood anxiety worldwide. Anxiety can have a serious, long-term negative impact on children and adolescents, so intervention in learning environments by school personnel is crucial. The first step toward helpful anxiety intervention is understanding anxiety itself, so this chapter:

- describes the target student population
- distinguishes anxiety that's a normal human experience from maladaptive anxiety
- defines anxiety
- outlines the key characteristics of anxiety
- explains the most common childhood anxiety disorders

Two Priorities: Prevention and Intervention

Two populations of children can benefit from prevention and intervention:

1. Some students demonstrate anxiety that interferes with their academic achievement and social relationships, but they aren't diagnosed with anxiety disorders. These children experience recurring fear, worry, and/or nervousness over circumstances in their lives or over future events. This anxiety may result in physiological, social, or performance-related challenges and may negatively affect their motivation (Killu and Crundwell 2016). Supporting these students with proactive interventions is key to preventing them from developing debilitating diagnosed anxiety disorders.

2. Some students have diagnosed anxiety disorders. An anxiety disorder is a neurobiological condition that is excessive, atypical, and demonstrated

> **THINK ABOUT IT**
> Think about these questions as you start reading chapter 1:
> - What does the word *anxiety* mean to you?
> - Were you anxious in school as a child or adolescent? How did that anxiety affect your relationships and behaviors?
> - Which of your students, if any, show signs of anxiety? What behaviors lead you to believe they have anxiety?

beyond the developmentally appropriate period (Killu and Crundwell 2016). These children are typically identified for special education or Section 504 services and have individualized education programs (IEPs) or 504 plans that outline a range of instructional and psychological services. Their unique needs are often met by special education teachers, school psychologists, counselors, and behavioral support professionals. The strategies in this book can be used by any teacher or school specialist who works with children who have diagnosed anxiety disorders, such as separation anxiety disorder, social anxiety disorder, or generalized anxiety disorder.

Preventing excessive anxiety in schools is critical. (To find out why, see chapter 4.) It's equally important to support students whose behaviors are consistent with anxiety disorders, regardless of whether they are diagnosed or receiving care from mental health professionals. Teachers are in a unique position to address students' mental well-being routinely. Yet most have little training or support in responding to children's anxiety in the classroom.

We recognize that many professionals who work with children do not have backgrounds in special education or psychology or may not have specialized training in helping children stay mentally well. Our experiences in schools tell us there is a notable gap between what teachers need—information and professional development on how to prevent and respond to childhood anxiety—and what they have received. This book aims to provide the background information on anxiety that teachers need coupled with intervention strategies that teachers can easily understand and use. We are committed to helping teachers meet students' needs regardless of their diagnosis or disability status.

IN THE RESEARCH

Behavior analyst and special educator Jessica Minahan explains: "Few teachers receive significant training in their teacher preparation programs in mental health and behavioral best practices. By and large, teachers are left on their own to learn about the effects of anxiety on learning and behavior and to figure out how to address it in the classroom" (2019, para. 1).

Minahan suggests that teachers can be instrumental in helping students deal with mental health issues if they are equipped to intervene. She explains: "The fact is that teachers come face-to-face with students' anxieties every day; they are in a position to provide support, in addition to outside therapists and school counselors, and they can do so effectively if they understand certain basic principles and strategies" (2019, para. 4).

Anxiety: A Normal Human Experience

Let's first think about anxiety as a normal human experience. In simple terms, anxiety is the brain responding to perceived danger. It is the brain's way of actively advising the rest of the body to avoid danger (Beesdo, Knappe, and Pine 2009). Anxiety serves to protect the human body and keep it alive long enough to pass on its genes to the next generation (Vallance and Fernandez 2016). Researchers find that anxiety is present in human infancy (Beesdo, Knappe, and Pine 2009) and that two- and three-year-old children naturally fear animals, which coincides with the time they begin to explore their surroundings (Vallance and Fernandez 2016).

All humans experience varying degrees of fear and worry throughout life. As an educator, you may experience anxiety when you're late for school, when your leadership team evaluates you, when you're in conflict with a parent, or when students behave unreasonably. Anxiety typically develops when you anticipate negative repercussions from an event or situation (Killu and Crundwell 2016). So, using the professional examples above, you may feel anxious because of the outcomes you anticipate: being reprimanded, performing poorly, quarreling with the parent, or having to work with defiant students. In your personal life, you may have deep fear and worry when a loved one is gravely ill, when you speak in front of large groups of people, when you interview for a job, or when you make large purchases, such as a home or car. In these instances, anxiety is a normal, expected human experience; it is not pathological or maladaptive. It is an adaptive state of arousal. This means you have predictable anxiety and are dealing with it accordingly (Killu and Crundwell 2016).

Children experience anxiety too, and some suffer from it from regularly. Some fears and worries are normal in the course of child development. At nine or ten months, for example, infants fear unfamiliar adults and become distressed or weary in their company (National Scientific Council on the Developing Child 2010). These emotions can carry over into early childhood; young children experience some hesitancy in greeting others they do not know. As children age and are exposed to various social circles, they learn that most adults do not pose threats, and this anxiety dissipates over time.

Children may experience anxiety over what they imagine in certain circumstances, such as monsters lurking in the dark, characters in films and books, such as wicked flying monkeys or villainous stepmothers, or specific animals or people, such as dogs or clowns. See the following table for examples of the common fears and worries people demonstrate at various ages. These anxieties peak between ages four and five. Children may act nervous and shy and avoid people, places, or situations that seem dangerous, but this degree of anxiety does not necessarily disrupt their lives (National Scientific Council on the Developing Child 2010; Bhatia and Goyal 2018) and is typically transitory (Burke 2007).

The Ages of Common Fears

Age of Child	Typical Fears
9 months to 3 years	sudden movements, loud noises, separation from caregivers, strangers
3 to 6 years	animals, the dark, monsters, ghosts
6 to 12 years	performance anxiety
12 to 18 years	social anxiety, fear of failure or rejection
adulthood	illness, death

Source: Vallance, Aaron K., and Victoria Fernandez. 2016. "Anxiety Disorders in Children and Adolescents: Aetiology, Diagnosis, and Treatment." *BJPsych Advances* 22 (5): 335–344. doi.org/10.1192/apt.bp.114.014183. Reproduced with permission.

When children feel anxiety, they may report any of a variety of physical complaints. For example, some may have headaches, stomachaches, nausea, vomiting, and diarrhea. Others may appear restless, fatigued, and irritable, and may have difficulty concentrating. Some children have recurrent, diffuse abdominal pain; tics; perspiration; flushed face; trembling; or incontinence.

Maladaptive Anxiety

Anxiety is considered maladaptive when it is excessive—out of proportion or unreasonable for the gravity or stress of the situation—and results in significant distress. Maladaptive anxiety is so severe and persistent that the anxious person engages in self-defeating behaviors that hinder daily functioning (Killu and Crundwell 2016). Some signs of excessive anxiety in children might be crying easily, throwing tantrums, avoiding play and social opportunities, having unreasonably high expectations for school performance, and freezing up when they are the focus of attention.

Consider how these anxiety-based behaviors might impact a student's performance in the classroom:

- A first grader cries throughout the morning because she fears something horrible will happen to her mother.
- A second grader will only work alone because they are scared that others will judge them harshly.
- A fourth grader refuses to speak out loud because he worries he will embarrass himself.
- A fifth grader cries hourly because she thinks her classmates are giving her mean looks.
- A sixth grader never accepts invitations to classmates' parties or outings because he fears socializing with people he doesn't know well.
- A seventh grader feels nauseated and shaky when they make errors on worksheets.
- An eighth grader refuses to eat lunch at school because she worries others will criticize the way she eats.

In these examples, each student's level of distress is significant and developmentally inappropriate, and it may become problematic if it is persistent, severe, and long-lasting.

Key Characteristics of Anxiety

Researchers have proposed many definitions of anxiety. We prefer one that describes feelings and behaviors related to everyday life—especially school—that teachers and counselors can use. Psychiatric researchers Aaron Vallance and Victoria Fernandez propose the following definition. It is especially useful because it discusses the various areas of functioning affected by anxiety (more on those in chapter 2): "Anxiety is an uncomfortable experience characterized by emotional (e.g., unease, distress), cognitive (e.g., fears, worries, helplessness), physiological (e.g., muscle tension), and behavioral (e.g., avoidance) changes. The anxious child commonly focuses on the future, fearful of danger, either specific or undefined" (2016, 335).

What's the difference between anxiety and fear? Anxiety is more commonly associated with cautious or avoidant behaviors, muscle tension, and vigilance in preparation for anticipated danger. In other words: anxiety is a reaction to a future threat. Fear is the emotional response to a real or perceived imminent threat with surges of autonomic arousal necessary for fight or flight such as pounding heart, sweating, or shaking; thoughts of immediate danger; and escape behaviors (American Psychiatric Association 2013). While anxiety and fear are distinct, they do overlap, and many experts view fear as a key feature of anxiety.

Anxious children often misinterpret situations, people, and objects as negative or threatening (Dias et al. 2016). As a result:

- They become overly afraid, which triggers an explosion of faulty thoughts, emotions, and behaviors.

- They overreact to perceived threats. For example, some anxious students might freeze when reading about make-believe villains.

- They misinterpret contexts (they may believe a rainstorm will destroy their home), people (adult-driven cargo vans hide kidnapped children), or things (trees come alive during storms and eat children).

Just as anxious children may overestimate seemingly dangerous situations, they may underestimate their ability to cope in anxiety-evoking situations. When something triggers their anxiety, they may have faulty, dysfunctional, or negative thoughts (cognitive distortions), and they tell themselves (and ruminate over) statements that are not true. As in the Swedish proverb, their worry gives small things big shadows.

Worry often gives a small thing a big shadow. —SWEDISH PROVERB

Note how these anxious thoughts tend to focus on negative social and physical outcomes:

I'm going to flunk the test and I'll never go to college.

I must have cancer because my body aches.

We're going to be in a bad car wreck, I just know it.

The dog next door wants to kill me.

They think I'm dumb.

They think I look funny.

They're going to laugh at me.

I'm not going to play with them because I'll get hurt.

Something horrible is going to happen to my mom.

Additionally, when anxious children feel threatened by a situation, they want to actively avoid it. When they cannot, they may appear hesitant, uncertain, withdrawn, and scared. Some may engage in ritualized actions, while others may feel sick or cry. For example, most children would find the offer of an afternoon with friends at an amusement park exciting, and they'd look forward to it eagerly. But children prone to anxiety may prefer to stay at home playing by themselves rather than risk socializing.

CLASSROOM CONNECTION

For many children with anxiety, uncertainty leads to worry and fear. When educators clearly define, teach, and consistently implement routines, students with anxiety can rely on the predictability of the school day. Establishing routines for beginning and ending activities, for transitioning from one setting to another, and for working collaboratively helps students with anxiety feel comfortable and secure in the classroom. After teaching basic routines, practice them and give regular reminders about what to expect. See action strategies 20 through 24 for how to make instructional routines and procedures more predictable.

Anxiety Disorders in Children

When anxiety is severe and persistent and negatively affects a child across settings, then it can develop into an anxiety disorder. When we use the term *anxiety disorder*, we are saying that anxiety is a neurological-biological condition. Anxiety disorder is an internalizing mental disorder. An internalizing disorder has symptoms that are cognitive and hard to observe. An externalizing disorder, by contrast, has symptoms that are expressed through behavioral excess and are thus easy to observe. In an overview of studies/research, Hurrell, Hudson, and Schniering point out that when children have an anxiety disorder, they "have less understanding of hiding and changing emotions, experience negative emotions more intensely, are more dysregulated in their expression of emotion, and engage in more maladaptive and fewer problem-solving emotion regulation strategies" (2015, 72).

Licensed psychiatrists and psychologists diagnose children with anxiety disorders using the *Diagnostic and Statistical Manual of Mental Disorders, Fifth Edition (DSM-5)*. The *DSM-5* contains a section on anxiety disorders that includes eleven distinct disorders. The disorders have related features and conditions, but they manifest in different ways. To be diagnosed with an anxiety disorder, a child must have had symptoms for a specified period and meet a certain number of listed criteria.

The *DSM-5* includes the following anxiety disorders:

- separation anxiety
- selective mutism
- specific phobia

- social anxiety disorder (social phobia)
- panic disorder
- generalized anxiety disorder
- agoraphobia
- substance- or medication-induced anxiety disorder
- anxiety disorder due to another medical condition
- other specified anxiety disorder
- unspecified anxiety disorder

Of these, separation anxiety disorder, generalized anxiety disorder, and social anxiety disorder are the most common anxiety diagnoses among children and adolescents (Yale Medicine 2023). We strongly recommend that you consult the *DSM-5* for a complete description of each anxiety disorder, but here are brief descriptions of the three most common in children.

Separation Anxiety Disorder

Children diagnosed with separation anxiety have debilitating worry about their parents' or other caregivers' welfare and stress excessively over being separated from them. This intense worry is atypical for their developmental age and shows up when children are separated from or threatened with separation from their caregivers. In most cases, the children fear or worry that something bad will happen to their parents when they are apart, and they may have outbursts at school when caregivers drop them off at the start of the day. Children may cry, throw tantrums, or have physical symptoms such as headaches, stomachaches, and nausea. Often, they worry throughout the day for their caregivers, ask repeatedly about them, and fear that caregivers will not pick them up after school. Children with separation anxiety disorder often have nightmares of being separated from their caregivers, refuse to separate even for sleepovers or visiting friends or relatives, and worry that their caregivers will be injured, hurt, killed, or kidnapped while they are separated.

Social Anxiety Disorder

Children diagnosed with social anxiety have excessive fear and worry over interacting with children and adults alike. Consequently, they avoid social situations to avoid embarrassing themselves or dealing with the discomfort of mingling with others. They might fear meeting children they do not know, talking to authority figures such as teachers or principals, giving presentations, and speaking in front of others.

Children with social anxiety are typically well-behaved, quiet, and reserved and have a limited group of friends. Unsurprisingly, they have a difficult time making and keeping friends. "It should be noted that socially anxious children are not necessarily poor in social skills. They are commonly ignored or neglected rather than rejected. However, as a result of their anxiety, they may sometimes act in a socially awkward manner and may perform poorly in social situations. For example, they may not speak very much or may talk very quietly, they may show poor eye contact, or they may talk in a hesitant and uncertain manner" (Rapee 2018, 4). Their anxiety can hinder their social skills development, resulting in potential social isolation.

Children with social anxiety are highly self-conscious or self-focused and mistakenly believe that they will behave in ways that are embarrassing or humiliating in the company of others. They tend to think that others will view them negatively—for example, as ugly, stupid, or odd—so they avoid being the center of attention at all costs. Moreover, as they misinterpret social situations negatively, they scrutinize their own social presentation and further exacerbate their anxiety.

Generalized Anxiety Disorder

Children diagnosed with generalized anxiety disorder have excessive and persistent worry over a wide range of everyday activities, situations, and events. Their concerns are not limited to one context or aspect of their lives; instead, they have multiple worries across life domains. They can worry over new and unfamiliar situations (such as having a substitute teacher), catastrophic events (such as the most recent storm), and health (such as not being able to breathe like everyone else), family (such as a parent who regularly works out of town), and social concerns (such as public protests). These children often find it hard to regulate their worries and may report physical symptoms such as restlessness, fatigue, sleep disturbance, and difficulty concentrating. At school, "academic demands often trigger excessive and persistent worries about performance and perfectionism. The students are often preoccupied with fears of making mistakes, failing, and disappointing their teachers, which negatively impair their classroom behavior, seeking reassurance often from their teacher" (Ginsburg et al. 2019, 1).

We hope that after reading this chapter, you feel well supplied with information that aids your teaching and your interactions with anxious students, both diagnosed and undiagnosed. Use the "Here's What. So What? Now What?" reflection form on the next page to review what you've learned, consider its implications, and articulate practices you might change. Perhaps you will try a new strategy, do something differently, or end a practice you've decided is unhelpful.

Here's What. So What? Now What?

Here's what. →

What did you learn about childhood and adolescent anxiety from reading chapter 1?

So what? →

What does this information mean to you, your students, and your learning community?

Now what? →

What can you do with this information? What changes in practice will you make?

CHAPTER 2

A Framework for Childhood Anxiety:
Prevalence, Effects, and Impacts on Functioning

Anxiety is a normal human emotion, but it can develop into a serious problem when it is excessive and leads to debilitating behaviors. An anxious child, whether diagnosed or not, typically focuses on and worries about the future and experiences emotional, cognitive, physiological, and behavioral symptoms. To help you recognize anxious children in your school or classroom, this chapter explores:

- the prevalence of anxiety in children and adolescents
- the effects of anxiety across the human lifespan
- how anxiety looks at various ages
- how anxiety affects functioning in four domains

Anxiety is not simply an emotional problem that causes nervousness, shyness, fear, or worry. Anxiety can hinder functioning in four domains: physiological, behavioral, social and emotional, and academic or cognitive. In a school setting, it is important for educators to recognize anxiety in each of these domains.

> **THINK ABOUT IT**
> Think about these questions as you start reading chapter 2:
> - How pervasive is anxiety in your school and in your classroom?
> - Which anxiety-related student behaviors concern you the most?
> - When a student has anxiety, what problems do you anticipate?

Prevalence

Childhood anxiety is a top public health concern because it is so widespread. Prevalence rates have been rising steadily, despite known underreporting and underdiagnosing. As we mentioned in the introduction, the rates of depression and anxiety have double compared to prepandemic estimates (Racine, McArthur, and Cooke 2021). Anxiety disorders are also the earliest forms of mental illness to emerge; that is, the onset of anxiety or any anxiety disorder typically happens during childhood.

In any given school population, 6 to 12 percent of students meet the diagnostic criteria for an anxiety disorder (Killu and Crundwell 2016). As mentioned in chapter 1, the most common diagnoses are separation anxiety disorder, generalized anxiety disorder, and social anxiety disorder (Yale Medicine 2023).

In terms of other demographic variables, research finds that girls outnumber boys in each anxiety disorder. In fact, girls are twice as likely to develop an anxiety disorder as boys are (Bhatia and Goyal 2018). Although there are no significant differences in the prevalence rates between boys and girls in childhood, the difference increases notably as children age; some studies find the difference as high as three girls to one boy (Beesdo, Knappe, and Pine 2009). The only time that studies found the prevalence of anxiety higher in boys was when they considered co-occurring autism spectrum disorder (ASD) and attention deficit hyperactivity disorder (ADHD) (Bitsko et al. 2018). Anxiety often co-occurs with ASD, ADHD, and oppositional defiant disorder (ODD); anxiety rates are as high as 84 percent in children with ASD (Vallance and Fernandez 2016).

When it comes to treatment for anxiety, fewer than 20 percent of young people with anxiety disorders access support, including specialized educational and mental health intervention (Hugh-Jones et al. 2020). Of those who receive treatment in the form of counseling or medication, most are White children who see mental health professionals at school or through an outpatient setting. Simply put, the need for effective, evidence-based counseling and therapy is far greater than what is available, and access is poor (Chavira et al. 2009; Ginsburg et al. 2019). As these statistics confirm, most children suffering from anxiety are underidentified and untreated. In fact, "as little as 1 percent of youth with anxiety seek treatment in the year their symptoms begin, and most anxiety symptoms go untreated for years" (Child Mind Institute 2018, 12).

CLASSROOM CONNECTION

Staying attuned to students' feelings is important, and many teachers have effective ways of checking in with students that do not compromise their privacy or confidentiality. If you are working with young students, you can observe and listen to your students during circle time, sharing time, or morning meetings. Pay special attention to signs of worry, fear, distress, sadness, or anxiety during these group times to note the frequency and severity of these emotions. For older students, teacher check-ins may be quick, one-on-one conversations outside the classroom door or while you move around to check on student work. You might also set up simple systems students can use to communicate privately, such as the Box of Worries in Action Strategy 15.

Across the Lifespan

Earlier, we explained that children with anxiety are at risk for serious academic, social, and emotional problems. Anxiety has immediate effects in the classroom; that is, stress hinders children's learning, memory, and social behavior. Anxiety-related problems aren't confined to childhood, though. Persistent childhood anxiety also causes long-term difficulties that last well into adulthood. Untreated childhood anxiety poses risks for serious challenges later in life. "Longitudinal research has shown that anxious children are at greater risk for anxiety, mood, and externalizing disorders in adolescence and for anxiety, mood, and substance use disorders as well as suicide in adulthood" (Rapee 2018, 6).

Another group of researchers noted that students with anxiety were at risk for depression, alcoholism, and antisocial behaviors later in life (Werner-Seidler et al. 2017). In fact, research evidence confirms that childhood anxiety increases the probability of engaging in risky social behavior and developing chronic health problems, including obesity and neurobehavioral conditions, in adolescence and adulthood. Researcher Rebecca Bitsko (2018) and her colleagues at the Centers for Disease Control and Prevention (CDC) also maintain that anxiety throughout the lifespan coincides with early mortality.

During childhood and adolescence, symptoms of anxiety can evolve from the mild to the transient to a diagnosed disorder. The typical progression of fear and anxiety in children unfolds as follows (Killu and Crundwell 2016; National Scientific Council on the Developing Child 2010):

- **In infancy:** Babies feel fear at six to twelve months old, mostly from unexpected loud noises such as barking dogs or loud trucks and unpredictable events such as a jack-in-the-box popping up. At nine to ten months, babies experience stranger anxiety, which means they react with wariness and distress when they encounter adults they do not know. Later in infancy, they may fear extreme novelty and heights.

- **In early childhood:** Toddlers and preschoolers express fear and anxiety over unfamiliar people, sleeping alone, thunderstorms, and the dark. The unease they feel toward people they don't know dissipates as they age and get to know a greater number of adults and children. At five years old, they may express fear over fancied malevolent characters, such as witches, zombies, and monsters, which corresponds to their growing imaginations. These fears dissipate by seven or eight years old. Nighttime fears are common in children between seven and nine years old; however, these fears start as young as three and are correlated with anxiety by age five (Reynolds and Alfano 2016).

- **In mid to late childhood:** Fears and anxieties typically subside. Children are maturing and can discern between what's real and what's imaginary and can exercise agency. Additionally, they have a much stronger sense of predictability in their surroundings. They know that monsters do not live in closets; they know they can turn off a scary movie or tell an adult about a hazardous circumstance; and they know they can depend on reliable adults and peers for support, encouragement, and companionship.

Here is an overview of typical age of onset for anxiety disorders in children who develop them:

- Animal phobias appear in early childhood, at six to seven years old.

- Separation anxiety begins between seven and nine years old, often when a child has difficulty separating from parents and staying at school all day.

- Specific phobias most often materialize before twelve years old. These may include fear of shots or doctors, the dark, sleeping alone, animals, death, and failure.

- Generalized anxiety disorder emerges around ten to twelve years old.

- Social anxiety develops in late childhood and early adolescence, around eleven to thirteen years.

- Specific anxiety disorders, such as agoraphobia, panic disorder, and obsessive-compulsive disorder, mostly emerge in adolescence.

Fears and anxiety typically diminish with age, especially when children live and attend school in safe and secure environments with warm and positive interactions, emotionally available adults, predictable routines, and supportive peers who offer reassurance and a sense of belonging. Fears and anxiety do not diminish when children live with recurring maltreatment and threatening circumstances, such as:

- physical, sexual, or emotional abuse

- emotional or physical neglect

- household dysfunction: parents divorced or separated, witnessing a family member being treated violently, a household member addicted to alcohol or other drugs, a household member suicidal or mentally ill, or household member incarcerated

> **IN THE RESEARCH**
> A good way to think about the shifts of anxiety by age is to think of anxiety from concrete, specific fears (a fear of dogs) to abstract worries (something could happen to my caregivers) to interpersonal concerns (I'll avoid my peers because they think I'm dumb anyway).

Child maltreatment occurs more often in families under stress. Financial insecurity and poverty make life unpredictable and therefore stressful. (Children may constantly wonder, "Where will we live next? Will we lose our car? Will we have electricity or water tomorrow? Will there be food when I get home?") About half of all children who live in poverty witness violence or are indirect victims of violence. In short, although anxiety disorders occur in urban, suburban, and rural communities at all socioeconomic levels, children who live in low-income households are more likely to develop an anxiety disorder than children who do not (McCarthy 2019).

Anxiety looks different in children of different ages. Young children with separation anxiety may seem fearful of leaving family members or caregivers. They may present general distress, physical complaints, and perfectionistic behaviors. Older children with anxiety tend to fear embarrassment or rejection. They might have difficulty initiating social interactions and making and keeping friends and may feel lonely and lacking in social worth. Adolescents and young adults with anxiety may experience restlessness, fatigue, irritability, difficulty concentrating, and sleep disturbance. A core feature of their anxiety is avoidance of situations, places, or stimuli, which can look like hesitancy, uncertainty, withdrawal, or ritualized activities. A threat or anticipation of a threat triggers the avoidance. The trigger, or precipitating event that leads to the avoidance, can vary.

Impacts on Functioning in Four Domains

Anxiety can hinder several key areas of functioning that are necessary for school success, and the behaviors present differently at different ages, as described. Students may demonstrate problems or limitations related to just one domain, or they may have pervasive anxiety issues that affect all four domains. When you understand the relationship between anxiety and school functioning, you can more quickly recognize students' anxiety-related issues and work to support those students. The key domains for children and adolescents are:

- physiological
- behavioral
- social and emotional
- academic or cognitive

THINK ABOUT IT

As you read about eight-year-old Ray, reflect on how his adverse experiences might contribute to his anxiety.

Sometimes Ray's mother is home after school; sometimes she isn't. Ray's older brother is in charge when their mother is absent. He teases Ray relentlessly, calling him ugly and a loser. When their mother's boyfriend comes around, he enjoys telling Ray that evil ghosts live in the abandoned house next door and makes him watch horror movies. Ray's mother has told him they might have to move out any day, because she is behind on their rent and electric bills. At school, Ray's teacher requires silence throughout the day and gives the students no time to socialize.

Physiological

Anxious children often report a range of physical ailments. They may complain about rapid heart rate, headaches, nausea, and muscle tension or experience visible tics of the eyelids or face, flushing of the skin, or vomiting. Some anxious children have difficulty sleeping. These physiological symptoms often lead to school absences that affect children's learning and academic performance, thus contributing to academic or cognitive symptoms.

Behavioral

Children with high levels of anxiety may appear restless and fidgety, may speak faster than normal, or may withdraw. They may also avoid lessons and classroom tasks like collaborative activities, may refuse to comply with directions, and may become irritable. Some children's refusal to participate may give the impression that they are oppositional. They may dodge questions, avoid asking for help, and refuse to work with others for fear of embarrassing themselves. Some anxious children appear quiet, reserved, and well-behaved. Adults should look for subtle changes in student behaviors that interfere with academic work and social relationships.

Social and Emotional

Students with anxiety may fail to make eye contact, be slow to interact with strangers, and seem shy or fearful. They may also refuse to explore new situations or adjust to changes. The US Department of Education report *Supporting Child and Student Social, Emotional, Behavioral, and Mental Health Needs* (2021) cites loneliness as a COVID-related emotional issue for many students and mentions changes in mood, isolation, and loss, all of which exacerbate anxiety.

Academic or Cognitive

Children with heightened anxiety may be unable to concentrate, attend to lessons, or solve problems, and they might have difficulty remembering content from prior lessons. They might expect to do poorly on assignments and tests; they may draw unfavorable academic comparisons with their peers ("They are all smarter than me."); they may express doubts about their abilities ("I can't read. I can't do math. I can't do anything."); and they may hold negative beliefs about the consequences of their academic abilities ("Everyone knows I'm stupid.").

Students with anxiety may also seem far more sensitive than other children when it comes to their academic performance. You might find them stressed about the quality of their work or preoccupied with making academic mistakes, failing tests and quizzes, and performing poorly at their sporting or musical events. They might agonize over disappointing their teachers, so they will seek perpetual reassurance from you and other school adults.

These four domains are not mutually exclusive. Children's anxiety symptoms can manifest consistently in one domain or may present across two or three or four domains. We have designed our action strategies to accommodate this reality. Some strategies address multiple domains simultaneously. For example, when a student is so anxious they withdraw and don't respond to requests to do their math assignment, this is both a physiological issue and an academic issue, and intervention addresses both domains. Likewise, a student with anxiety may have a social and emotional difficulty like making friends at lunch, and this may become a behavioral issue if the student is teased or bullied and becomes angry. Teacher intervention in the social and emotional domain also addresses the behavioral domain.

Downward Spirals

When children have heightened anxiety, a harmful downward spiral involving the four domains can develop.

Academic Downward Spiral

- First, a child's anxiety may make it impossible to concentrate, draw connections between lessons, and organize work.
- This lapse of cognitive efficiency hinders the child's work, further exacerbating their anxiety, especially when they compare their skills and abilities with those of other children in the classroom.

- This increased anxiety can lead to greater cognitive challenges, making it even harder for the child to attend to lessons.

- These difficulties then lead to decreased motivation that affects the child's performance, adding more stress.

Learned helplessness can develop from this spiral. Anxiety interferes with a student's concentration and performance, so they start to avoid difficult tasks. This leads to a tendency to give up quickly, and then self-blame and worry about competence. Eventually, the student's motivation and effort decrease, which hinders academic achievement and skill development.

Social Downward Spiral

Anxious children often have a hard time interacting with others, which can make establishing friendships challenging. Some children may be able to handle only one or two friends and a small circle of peers at the most. They may struggle with approaching some peers and fitting in with those they don't know well. Some anxious children will avoid social gatherings altogether because they fear others will reject or judge them harshly. They may think, "They're not going to like me," "They think I'm stupid," and "They're way cooler than me" whenever they are around their peers. These kinds of inaccurate, negative internal messages may be so overwhelming that anxious children prefer to skip social events and avoid social circles no matter how enticing these might seem to other students. Hayley Greenwood (2017), a young adult who has anxiety, describes it this way: "Living with anxiety is like being followed by a voice. It knows all your insecurities and uses them against you."

> ## "Living with anxiety is like being followed by a voice. It knows all your insecurities and uses them against you." —HAYLEY GREENWOOD

Alternatively, another sort of social downward spiral may develop. When anxious children believe their peers will judge them negatively, they may prefer to withdraw rather than interact with their classmates. As a result, they get fewer opportunities to practice applying social norms (such as knowing the right way to greet others or how much personal space to give them) and interpreting cues (such as body language that says, "I'm ready for this conversation to end").

Developing social skills suitable for interacting with peers is critical for children. But poor social skills combined with involuntary behaviors such as fidgeting or tics may repel peers. When anxious children are unable to use slang correctly, talk about the latest trends, and interpret social nuances—and they also have awkward manners that annoy or irritate others, like avoiding eye contact, dominating conversations, and talking solely about themselves, their peers may sneer at, ignore, or exclude them from social activities.

Some anxious children who have inadequate social skills may experience added stress, particularly if they desire interpersonal interactions. But others may function easily without acquaintances, especially if they do not long for or experience satisfaction from friendships. Either way, without stable peer relationships, anxious children can develop a low self-concept that is matched with ample doses of self-criticism. As a result, they may pick up a harmful habit of judging most social situations as unpredictable or dangerous—even those that are predictable and safe—that intensifies their anxiety and increases the probability of further social isolation.

IN THE RESEARCH

Killu and Crundwell describe the cycle of negative social functioning in anxious children this way: "By avoiding social interactions with their peers, social skill development is inhibited and social skill deficits may become so pronounced that they subsequently impact their ability to interact with others, particularly in regard to eliciting positive social support from others" (2016, 32).

Use the "Here's What. So What? Now What?" reflection form on the next page to review what you've learned in this chapter, consider its implications, and articulate practices you might change.

Here's What. So What? Now What?

Here's what. →

What did you learn about childhood and adolescent anxiety from reading chapter 2?

So what? →

What does this information mean to you, your students, and your learning community?

Now what? →

What can you do with this information? What changes in practice will you make?

CHAPTER 3

Causes of Childhood Anxiety and Biological Stress Responses:
The Brains of Anxious Children

Childhood anxiety is widespread, and most young people with anxiety are underidentified and untreated. Untreated anxiety can have lasting effects well into adulthood. Anxiety presents in distinct ways in infancy, childhood, and adolescence, progressing from concrete specific fears to abstract worries to interpersonal concerns. Without intervention, this anxiety may escalate and causes academic and social downward spirals. To help you understand how specific interventions positively affect students' behavior in the classroom, this chapter explains:

- the causes of anxiety
- reasons why anxiety persists
- the potential biological stress responses

Causes of Anxiety

Scientists have identified four types of causes of anxiety: genetic, temperamental, psychosocial, and environmental (Killu and Crundwell 2016).

Genetic Causes

Some children are at high risk for anxiety simply because they are genetically predisposed to it. Research has found that general anxiety exists within families and is passed from one generation to the next (Killu and Crundwell 2016). Research also shows that "first-degree relatives of people with anxiety disorders are at increased risk to also have anxiety as well as mood disorders" (Rapee 2018, 8). In fact, nearly a third of anxiety is presumed to have some genetic connection.

THINK ABOUT IT
Think about these questions as you start reading the chapter:

- When have you seen your students experience anxiety?
- How did their anxiety manifest in your classroom?
- What do you think causes their anxiety?

Temperamental Causes

Temperament is a person's personality or disposition—their unique way of responding to new or unexpected situations. As most professionals who work with children and adolescents can attest, some children respond well to stress, while others fall apart when their routine or environment changes—even in a small way. Children who are behaviorally inhibited, extremely shy, easy criers, and inclined to withdraw, as well as children who tend to blame themselves for unfavorable events, are at risk for developing anxiety.

Psychosocial Causes

Psychosocial causes involve both psychological factors (thoughts and behaviors) and social factors (interactions and relationships with others). When children believe they have no control over their experiences, or their experiences generate persistent anxious emotions, they are more likely to develop anxiety. Studies have found that significant adverse experiences in childhood, such as the death of a parent, parental divorce, and physical and sexual abuse, can lead to an anxiety disorder (Beesdo, Knappe, and Pine 2009). Anxiety may not necessarily be caused by one specific event. "Isolated events have less direct effects over time; instead, it is the cumulative effect of multiple events that leads to the development of cognitive and affective patterns of anxiety" (Killu and Crundwell 2016, 31).

Environmental Causes

Children's risk for anxiety is also rooted in home life—specifically, how caregivers parent (Do they regularly scream at their children?), the behaviors caregivers model (Do they have public outbursts?), how caregivers prompt their children (Do they nag, scold, and punish?), and how caregivers reinforce anxiety and associated behaviors (Do they reinforce their children's fears?). Some studies have found that children with anxiety disorders have parents who do not talk about emotions, discourage their children from talking about their emotions, and have a less positive interaction style than parents of children without anxiety disorders (Hurrell, Hudson, and Schniering 2015). Other studies report similar results: parents who overcontrol their children or do not communicate effectively with them tend to keep anxious symptoms active in children. One study found an increased risk of social phobia in children whose parents overprotect or reject them (Beesdo, Knappe, and Pine 2009). Interestingly, one study noted that children mirror their mothers' anxiety. "Women's role is still more oriented to family than men's, which promotes the existence of 'proximity space' where children possibly perceive and share mothers' anxiety experiences. . . . In this sense, children are vulnerable to their mothers' anxiety" (Dias et al. 2016, 8).

Also, as we mentioned in chapter 2, living in underresourced communities, in high-crime communities, and neighborhoods that force residents to live in social isolation may all contribute to children's anxiety. Finally, some children's overscheduled lives cause them anxiety. They are involved in so many after- and outside-of-school activities that they have little or no downtime to rest, unwind, and calm down.

Why Anxiety Persists

Anxiety can become conditioned in children, which means that children get anxious over a harmless stimulus simply because it resembles an earlier aversive stimulus. Conditioned behaviors are patterns that can be difficult to interrupt, which is why teachers play such an important role in changing the dynamics of pattern. Consider sixth grader Joaquin, who is anxious at school because several teachers and coaches there have beards just like his father, who abandoned the family months ago in a drunken rage. Any man at school who looks or sounds like his father or has a similar manner could trigger Joaquin's anxiety. "For young children who perceive the world as a threatening place, a wide range of conditions can trigger anxious behaviors that then impair their ability to learn and to interact socially with others" (National Scientific Council on the Developing Child 2010, 3). This suggests that even children who have the nicest teachers with the most welcoming classrooms might experience recurring anxiety because of a teacher's hairstyle, scent, clothing, classroom color, teaching materials, or any other sensory details.

Simply living in the modern world causes some children anxiety. "Children and teens have great access to an extensive amount of social media that barrage them daily with images and reports of death, doom and disaster around the world, further raising feelings of anxiety" (Schaefer and Drewes 2018, 4). Additionally, many children become aware of sexual abuses, violent crimes, and drug abuses at young ages through media. Some children sense that they are living in a dangerous world, and this is a constant source of stress for them. Because they lack the skills to deal with anxiety on their own, this stress persists.

School itself can be stressful and anxiety inducing. Many children have challenges at school that are difficult to navigate. Young children, for example, have to adapt to leaving the comforts of home and family for full days; they have to work on establishing relationships with teachers and specialists; and they have to master making and keeping friends. As they mature and their identities develop, they begin to ponder their status among their peers. They might become anxious from appraising their own popularity, how they fit in, how they can break into specific social circles, and how to avoid social faux pas. Adolescents often stress over their appearance and must sometimes cope with peer pressure to engage in risky behaviors such as smoking, drug use, and sexual activity.

Additionally, many school districts are required to prepare school personnel and children for dealing with armed intruders. Routine drills are designed to protect children from harm, but these drills cause some children anxiety as they barricade themselves, run to secure spaces, and watch anxiety increase in their teachers and peers. Adolescents may have to enter school through metal detectors and entrances that are monitored by school resource officers, which suggest that danger could erupt at any moment.

The Stress Response System and Its Relationship to Anxiety

The human stress response system is a process in which information is received by the senses and travels through the peripheral nerves and spinal cord to the limbic system in the brain, and the brain reacts. The limbic system is a group of interconnected brain structures that includes the amygdala, hippocampus, thalamus, and hypothalamus. The hippocampus and prefrontal cortex receive sensory signals simultaneously.

The hippocampus is a processing hub and storage bank for memories. When it receives a signal, it messages the amygdala to determine if the signal has a "danger" memory association. The amygdala is considered the alarm center of the brain. Without conscious awareness, it assesses the environment based on memory of similar circumstances and weighs the threat level of a stimulus, person, or event.

The prefrontal cortex is known as the decision-making region of the brain. It is responsible for regulating emotions. It manages executive functioning properties such as the following:

- making, following, and altering plans
- controlling and focusing attention
- inhibiting impulsive behavior
- developing the ability to hold and incorporate new information in decision making

If the amygdala determines that the environment connects to a memory that poses no or low threat, the prefrontal cortex moderates the limbic system. So, in no- or low-danger circumstances, the prefrontal cortex can reason, rationalize, solve problems, and apply other executive functioning skills. In other words, children can learn.

However, if the amygdala determines that the environment connects to a threatening memory, it signals the adrenal glands to secrete the hormones epinephrine and cortisol to launch a fight, flight, freeze, or fawn stress response. (For more on fight, flight, freeze, or fawn, see page 39.) In his book *Brain Rules,* molecular biologist John Medina explains that this stress response system served to protect prehistoric humans from physical danger: "The saber-toothed tiger either ate us or we ran away from it— or a lucky few might stab it, but the whole thing was usually over in moments. Consequently, our stress

CLASSROOM CONNECTION

When the environment is in disarray or when students have too many choices, they may have difficulty focusing and making decisions. This is especially true of children and adolescents with anxiety disorders. Organizing the classroom furniture, seating, and materials in a clear and user-friendly way helps students quickly become familiar with the setting. When they know where things are and how to access them, where to sit, and how to move around the classroom, it reduces uncertainty and worry. Display visual schedules with signals for transitions, provide transparent plastic bins for materials, use consistent methods for giving directions, and teach students how to work together. When these basics are in place, students can stress less and learn more.

responses were shaped to solve problems that lasted not for years, but for seconds. They . . . get our muscles moving us as quickly as possible out of harm's way" (2014, 63).

When children have elevated stress, the prefrontal cortex's capacity is suppressed. In fact, the more anxious the child is, the stronger the signal is from their amygdala to subdue the prefrontal cortex. One team of mental health researchers found that "higher levels of anxiety were associated with less positive initial reactions to aversive images, less ability to regulate emotional reaction in response to aversive images, and more impulsive reactions during reappraisal of aversive images. Higher stress reactivity was linked with less controlled, more impulsive reactions when reappraising aversive images, suggesting the dorso-lateral prefrontal cortex is less able to carry out its job" (Digitale 2021, para. 12).

> **IN THE RESEARCH**
> Persistent fear and anxiety in childhood can impair the architecture of the growing brain, especially during sensitive periods of development (National Scientific Council on the Developing Child 2010). The limbic system and the prefrontal cortex develop in ways that do not function as effectively in children who experience recurring stress as in children who do not.

In short: in a state of heightened stress, the amygdala blocks the prefrontal cortex from doing its job of rational thinking. Some trauma experts call this the amygdala hijack. "In fact, the wiring is so efficient that the amygdala and hypothalamus start this cascade even before the brain's visual centers have had a chance to fully process what is happening. That's why people are able to jump out of the path of an oncoming car even before they think about what they are doing" (Harvard Health Publishing 2020, para. 8).

Let's look at two examples to illustrate what happens in the brain when two children see their fathers under different circumstances. The same stimulus is happening to both children, but their responses are dramatically different:

- Janessa sees her father with open arms and inclined for a hug. Her limbic system registers that he is not a threat, because she sees her father every afternoon when he picks her up from school, and it is always a safe interaction. As they walk home together, they make plans for dinner. Her prefrontal cortex reasons that it is completely safe to run to her father and hug him. She can focus her attention on her father, tell him what she learned at school that day, and plan for what they can eat later.

- Joaquin sees his father with open arms and inclined for a hug. Joaquin's limbic system registers that his father is a high threat because he has not seen his father in months, his father beat him the last time he was home, and his father told him that he plans to take him away from his mother when their divorce is finalized. Joaquin's amygdala triggers his adrenal glands to secrete epinephrine and cortisol to launch his stress response to this danger. So, Joaquin may fight his father (scream, punch, kick), flee from him (run away), freeze (stiffen and go silent), or fawn (say "You're the best dad!"). At the same time, Joaquin's prefrontal cortex is suppressed, so he cannot use his executive functioning skills effectively.

Imagine what happens when children have persistent fear and anxiety for much of their lives. What if Joaquin has heightened stress throughout the day, week, or month? What if he has anxiety when he sees his father, when his teacher yells (which happens daily), and when he wonders whether he can keep up academically with his peers? Under such elevated stress, it would be difficult for Joaquin to incorporate new information during class activities, finish work, be creative, suppress his impulses, and so forth. He would likely fall behind.

How Conditioning Leads to Generalized Anxiety

In some children, fear and anxiety become conditioned. That is, children become fearful or anxious over a neutral person, context, or item that happens to share some characteristic(s) of a threatening person, place, or thing. "Children who have had chronic and intense fearful experiences often lose the capacity to differentiate between threat and safety. This impairs their ability to learn and interact with others, because they frequently perceive threat in familiar social circumstances, such as on the playground or in school" (National Scientific Council on the Developing Child 2010, 5).

Let's take the example of third grader Amanda, who has anxiety because her mother has repeatedly told her that she doesn't know how much longer they will live in their house because she is behind on the rent and cannot keep up with the bills. Her mother has even said that she hopes that the Child Protective Services agency doesn't take Amanda away. At home, Amanda's stress response is triggered when:

- A city electricity truck parks outside her home. Then her electricity is cut off.
- Cardboard boxes appear on her doorstep. Amanda's mother instructs her to start packing because they are moving to an apartment, which will be smaller and cheaper.
- A man in a suit wearing horn-rimmed glasses knocks at the door. He's from Child Protective Services and wants to assess whether Amanda's mother can provide for her. He outlines what her mother is required to do by his next visit.
- A woman with long blonde hair shows up at the door. She's from a repossession company. She aggressively asks Amanda's mother for a payment to keep the family car.
- A special ringtone alerts her mother when the landlord is calling. It rings repeatedly over the weekend because he wants to know exactly when they will be out of the house.

Amanda may come to school with heightened anxiety. She may react with fear and anxiety at school when:

- A city electricity truck parks in front of the school building.
- Cardboard boxes of books appear on her classroom table.
- The assistant principal, who wears a suit and horn-rimmed glasses, visits her classroom.

- The school librarian, who has long blonde hair, walks by her classroom.
- Her teacher uses the same ringtone her mother uses for the landlord.

In this state of alertness and stress, Amanda would have a difficult time managing impulsivity, thinking flexibly, solving problems, applying past knowledge to new information, and so on, largely because she is in a nearly constant state of stress. At any given moment, she might be reacting to a stimulus that seems threatening by crying, talking, screaming, throwing a tantrum, running out of the classroom, or refusing to listen or comply.

Of course, it's difficult to predict what might trigger children like Amanda, given the many variables that can negatively affect a child's daily life. That's why it's critical to use classroom practices that promote feelings of safety, security, and trust. Even when such practices are implemented, it is still important to recognize some general triggers that often launch stress responses, such as loud or chaotic environments, physical touches, authority figures, imposed limits ("You have three minutes to put away your materials"), unpredictable schedules, or anyone wearing a uniform.

THINK ABOUT IT

Now that you have read about the relationships among the brain, stress, and anxiety, think about these questions:

- What triggers you to become anxious?
- How do you react when you feel anxious?
- What do you think triggers your students to react defensively, withdraw, become aggressive, or demonstrate other behaviors related to anxiety?

What to Expect When Anxiety Takes Over

Children who have continuous anxiety may construe ambiguous social situations negatively and/or catastrophize mildly negative social contexts. Thoughts that fixate on negative outcomes, both social and physical, are sometimes called threat beliefs or maladaptive thinking patterns. When children are emotionally distressed, they make information-processing errors:

- Anxious children make faulty assumptions about social contexts. Their beliefs about others are often inaccurate, negative, and dysfunctional. For example, when two sixth graders are laughing at lunch, sixth grader Alexis assumes they are the butt of the joke. When a student rolls his eyes over another student's comment, Alexis believes the comment is about them. A group of students huddled at an outside bench prompts suspicions of a conspiracy against Alexis.

- Anxious children don't realize when situations are not as dangerous as they seem. For example, fifth grader Michael assumes that his mother has been in a horrific car accident when she is late to pick him up. He believes his neighbor hates him because he thinks she gives him dirty looks whenever he's outside. (She doesn't.) And he thinks that his father is going to die from cancer because he's been to the doctor three weeks in a row (for a routine checkup, bloodwork, and follow-up visit).

■ Anxious children spend considerable time thinking about how they come across to others. They spend more time engaged in negative self-thoughts and feelings and less time contemplating other people's actual behaviors and responses. They continually self-monitor and use negative self-talk. They avoid social situations because they don't want to embarrass themselves; they fear others will judge them as weak, dumb, or boring; or they want to avoid showing signs of anxiety such as blushing, sweating, or stammering. For example, third-grader Araceli believes that the other students in her class think she is dumb. When the teacher assigns small groups to work on a project, Araceli watches the other students and assumes they are dismayed to be in her group. She feels embarrassed, flushes, and then withdraws. She hangs her head and makes no eye contact with anyone in her group. After a while, the other students stop trying to engage her, because she will not respond.

Persistent fear and anxiety during early life affect how children with anxiety regulate themselves as they age. Unsurprisingly, children with regular doses of heightened stress do not develop healthy patterns of emotional regulation. Their brains have not developed to self-regulate effectively, so they might:

■ **Fight:** Children might yell at you, call you names, curse at you, act silly, or refuse to talk or comply with your requests. They might have clenched fists, racing hearts, and grinding teeth, and they are ready to hit, kick, or shout.

■ **Flee:** Flight is a common response. Children might run out of the classroom, hide under a desk, put their heads down, or retreat in some other way. They feel trapped and want to escape.

■ **Freeze:** Children may withdraw from the class and pay no attention to you, their classmates, or authority figures. They may stop talking, stiffen, or tremble. They want to be alone.

■ **Fawn:** Children may give in to their peers, overapologize, or cling to you or a peer. They want to please everyone and may overcompliment others and ask them many questions.

We hope that after reading this chapter, you've gained a solid understanding of the causes of anxiety and what happens in the brain and the rest of the body when anxiety takes over. Use the "Here's What. So What? Now What?" reflection form on the next page to review what you've learned, consider its implications, and articulate practices you might change.

THE NEUROSCIENCE OF ANXIETY

If you want to dive deeper into the neuroscience of anxiety, the following books offer comprehensive explorations of the brain's complexity:

■ Neuroscience: *Exploring the Brain, Enhanced Fourth Edition* by Mark Bear, Barry Connors, and Michael A. Paradiso (Jones & Bartlett Learning, 2020)

■ *The Brain: The Story of You* by David Eagleman (Vintage Books, 2017)

■ *Brain & Behavior: An Introduction to Behavioral Neuroscience, Sixth Edition* by Bob Garrett and Gerald Hough (SAGE Publications, 2022)

■ *Your Brain, Explained: What Neuroscience Reveals about Your Brain and Its Quirks* by Marc Dingman (Nicholas Brealey Publishing, 2019)

Here's What. So What? Now What?

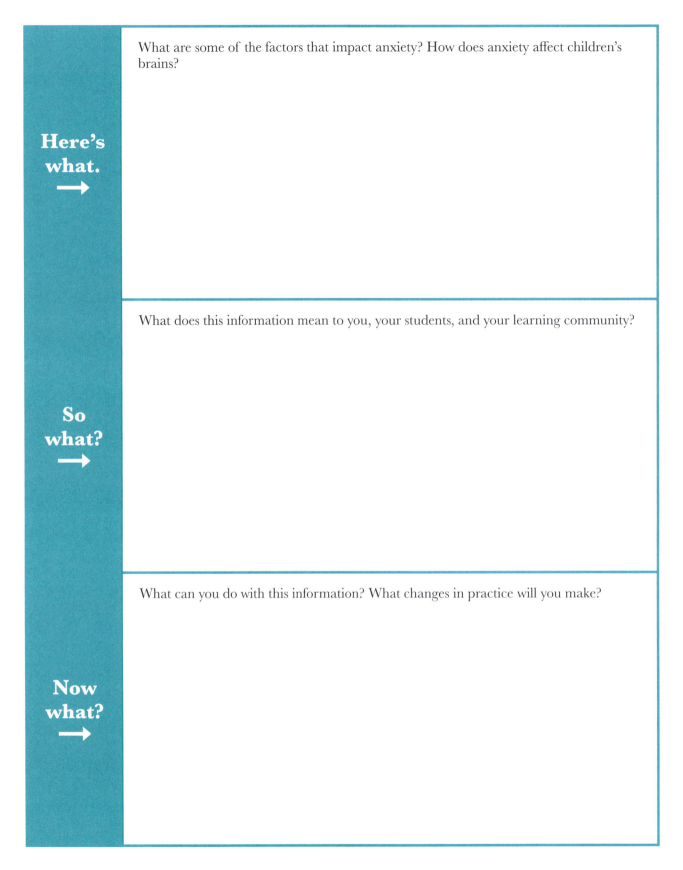

Here's what. →

What are some of the factors that impact anxiety? How does anxiety affect children's brains?

So what? →

What does this information mean to you, your students, and your learning community?

Now what? →

What can you do with this information? What changes in practice will you make?

CHAPTER 4

Addressing Childhood Anxiety in School:
School-Based Interventions, Programs, and Social and Emotional Learning

Understanding the biological aspects of anxiety—its causes, why it persists, and the potential physical stress responses—can help you understand why some children behave the way they do when they are anxious and how specific interventions positively affect students' behavior in the classroom. To build your understanding of school-based interventions, this chapter explains:

- why school-based intervention programs are critical for anxious students

- what types of school programs are available for students with anxiety

- what cognitive behavioral therapy (CBT) is and how its components can be implemented in schools

- how social and emotional learning (SEL) in classrooms improves children's mental health, socialization, academic achievement, and ability to cope with stressful life events

The Importance of School-Based Programs

The earlier the onset of anxiety disorders, the worse the prognosis. If left untreated, childhood anxiety can lead to negative and harmful outcomes: poor academic achievement and socialization, drug and alcohol abuse, risky sexual behavior, suicide risk, and physical health problems (Werner-Seidler et al. 2017). Preventive interventions not only thwart these poor outcomes, they are more cost-effective and less

THINK ABOUT IT

Think about these questions as you start reading the chapter:

- What interventions are used for anxious students in your school?

- How were the interventions selected?

- How effective are the interventions?

- What challenges do you face in implementing interventions for anxious students?

labor-intensive than waiting until students' anxiety-related behaviors are severe and frequent.

The introduction of this book discusses the advantages of teacher-provided strategies for preventing anxiety and intervening when children already demonstrate anxious behaviors. Of course, schools are not therapy clinics or hospitals. But schools not only are appropriate settings for anxiety prevention and intervention, they also have some important advantages:

- **Children are already at school for learning.** While individual and group counseling may be available to some students outside school, these opportunities are inaccessible to many students because of cost, logistical difficulties, and work constraints. In addition, some parents may not see the value of therapy.

- **School interventions are cost-effective.** For students whose families have little or no medical coverage or transportation, school offers a free and ready-made resource. Schools often are the institutions that connect a whole community and are the one resource that's familiar and accessible to all families.

- **Preventive interventions can be integrated into the school day.** Because school personnel deal with anxiety-related behaviors in many students throughout the day, they can intervene naturally, in the context of typical classroom or counseling activities. For students who don't want to call attention to their anxiety, an integrated approach can ensure accessibility with some anonymity—especially when universal approaches are delivered to all students. Programs provided at school can serve to normalize treatment and promote positive attitudes about it.

- **School is a main entry point into the mental health service system for young people.** Schools provide 70 percent of mental health treatment for children and adolescents (National Center for School Mental Health 2020). Schools are already supporting students' mental health, so it's important that school personnel have the tools they need to do so effectively.

School-Based Interventions and Programs

As chapter 2 discussed, childhood anxiety can hinder functioning in four domains: physiological, behavioral, social and emotional, and academic or cognitive. Educators may see anxiety-related behaviors and limitations in one or more of these domains. Keep in mind that each student expresses and experiences anxiety uniquely, so an intervention that works for one student might not work for another. For example, two students may be experiencing anxiety because their parents are divorcing. One may be quiet and stoic in class, refusing to socialize with peers (a freeze stress response), while the other may take any opportunity to escape from the classroom or the school (a flight stress response). Because anxiety-related behaviors vary widely, it might take several attempts to design effective intervention plans for individual students—and each plan will likely be unique.

Decades-long research on childhood anxiety shows that some interventions—now considered standard practices—contribute to students' academic and social progress, well-being, and emotional growth. The two most common types of interventions for childhood anxiety are medication (selective serotonin reuptake inhibitors, or SSRIs) and cognitive behavioral therapy (CBT). Medications are prescribed only by physicians, so this removes them as an option for most school-based programs. CBT is a type of psychological talk therapy. It may be offered to students and their families as a therapy outside of school, but it is typically not available in school unless it is a required service for students with identified disabilities. Students' individualized education programs (IEPs) may include counseling such as meeting with a social worker for an informal weekly check-in that uses key CBT components.

IN THE RESEARCH

Whether all students receive universal interventions (a whole class learns breathing exercises, for instance) or interventions are targeted to specific students who have risk factors or show mild symptoms (like helping a student reframe their thinking), preventive anxiety interventions lead to lasting benefits (Werner-Seidler et al. 2017):

- They prevent new cases of anxiety and reduce the incidence of anxiety disorder.

- They delay the onset of clinically significant symptoms of anxiety, which may make the disability less severe.

- They offer a way to avoid more intensive interventions later.

- They reverse anxiety-related behaviors if young children receive interventions before they have developed rigid patterns of behavior. In other words, interventions produce better results when they're provided early.

- They have the potential to produce prolonged meaningful improvements.

Cognitive Behavioral Therapy

A large body of research demonstrates the successful use of CBT for treating childhood anxiety disorders. For example, one review of twenty-four scientific studies focused on treating anxiety and depression with CBT concluded that individual and group therapies resulted in favorable effects, and follow-up data showed that the effects lasted for several years (In-Albon and Schneider 2007). Another study evaluating twenty-seven anxiety treatments and programs noted that "the case for CBT for treating childhood anxiety disorders is particularly strong" (Schwartz et al. 2019, 109). Still another study, which followed children for three years after CBT treatment, showed that CBT should be the "first-line psychosocial treatment for youths with anxiety disorders" because "CBT has been demonstrated to be effective in decreasing anxiety symptoms and facilitating remission of generalized anxiety disorder (GAD), separation anxiety disorder (SAD), and/or social anxiety disorder in children and adolescents" (Lee et al. 2016, 183).

The goals of CBT include (Wehry et al. 2015):

- teaching children with anxiety and their caregivers (or significant adults, such as educators) about its psychoeducational nature

- teaching children with anxiety how to manage their physiological reactions to anxiety

- helping children with anxiety identify their triggers, then teaching them how to restructure their thinking

- teaching anxious children problem-solving skills so they can better cope with inevitable challenges

- gradually exposing children with anxiety to triggers in ways that allow children to deal effectively with them and subsequently regulate themselves

- creating an alternative plan that children with anxiety can use when the original strategy is not as effective as expected

Traditionally, licensed psychotherapists conduct CBT systematically over six or eight weeks. Sometimes, children are taking prescribed medication while they are involved in CBT. Parents often participate in CBT sessions with their children.

While family and individual therapy, including CBT, are often effective for students with anxiety, these types of therapy aren't easily accessible. Few, if any, mental health specialists are available in many communities, and therapy may simply cost too much. In addition, it is highly unlikely that school professionals (whether counselors, psychologists, or clinical social workers) have the time or resources to provide CBT to all the students who would benefit from it. Of course, teachers are ideal service providers because they interact daily and consistently with students who have anxiety. But they lack the specialized training, credentials, time, and expertise to provide CBT.

CBT in School Interventions

However, there is one positive development: components of CBT are already being used successfully in classrooms and schools. Because CBT components can be taught individually, they can be adapted and used with students at school. Strategies such as cognitive restructuring, relaxation techniques, and positive self-talk are practical, easy to implement, and inexpensive. For example, deep breathing is a strategy that benefits all students, involves little or no cost, and can be taught by almost any classroom teacher, counselor, or school mental health specialist.

The action strategies in the second half of this book are interventions designed for students with anxiety. Many of them include one or more CBT components and are practical for use in classroom or counseling settings, whether for individual students, small groups, or a whole class. The components are as follows:

1. **Exposure** helps people confront their fears by gradually experiencing situations (for example, airplane flights) or things (such as spiders) that cause them distress.

2. **Modeling** is a technique in which people learn new behaviors by observing and imitating someone doing those behaviors. For example, a child who is anxious and fearful of doctors could watch another child who is not anxious calmly enter a clinic and approach a physician.

3. **Self-monitoring** occurs when people observe and sometimes record their own thoughts, emotions, body sensations, and behaviors. For example, a child could write about the thoughts and emotions they have when they hyperventilate. Self-monitoring can help people become aware of their own behavior and how they interact with their environment.

4. **Relaxation** is a process for calming down and exerting control over physical and mental tension. Relaxation can moderate breathing and reduce discomfort in the body as well as negative thinking.

5. **Cognitive restructuring** is a technique that helps people identify and interrupt negative or irrational thoughts and then redirect them. For example, you could teach a child who is preoccupied with a parent's well-being the mantra *Mom is at work and she is fine—I should focus on my work too.*

6. **Visualization** is forming mental pictures in the mind and using them to plan and mentally rehearse steps for appropriately approaching a problem, uncomfortable emotion, or irrational thought.

7. **Mindfulness** is consciously attending to one's thoughts, body sensations, and emotions, as well as controlling automatic reactions to them. Using breathing exercises to react to stressful situations calmly and positively is an example of mindfulness.

8. **Rehearsal** is visualizing and practicing interpersonal behaviors, responses, and skills to prepare for using them in real-life situations. For example, before a live performance, you might have a child stand on a stage with a microphone and visualize an audience.

 The action strategies that integrate one or more of these CBT components are flagged with this symbol.

School-Based Intervention Programs

Much of the research on school-based intervention programs for anxiety has examined those managed by counselors, psychologists, and social workers rather than lessons and activities used by individual teachers in the classroom. This happens for a few reasons: First, intervention programs can be standardized, or implemented according to specific protocols that articulate the number and length of individual sessions, the training required of the interventionist, and any conditions needed to ensure fidelity to the program requirements. Second, the outcomes of an intervention program can be measured and, in some cases, compared to a control group of students who did not participate in the program. Third, grouping students with similar anxiety-related issues and giving them support together can save time and resources.

Here are some of the better-known, research-based anxiety intervention programs for children and adolescents (* denotes a CBT treatment program):

- Cool Kids Anxiety Program (for ages seven to seventeen)*

- Baltimore Child Anxiety Treatment Study in the Schools (for ages seven to seventeen)*

- Cognitive-Behavioral Intervention for Trauma in Schools (for grades five through twelve)*

- Skills for Academic and Social Success (for adolescents who have social anxiety disorder)*

- Coping and Promoting Strength (for children ages six to thirteen of anxious parents)*

- Strongest Families Institute (Chase Worries Away for ages six to eleven, Defeat Anxiety for ages twelve to seventeen, Chase Pain Away for ages nine to sixteen)

- Cool Little Kids Plus Social Skills (for ages three to six)

- Timid to Tiger (for parents of children ages three to nine)*

> **CLASSROOM CONNECTION**
>
> Music is often a great stress reducer. Some doctors even suggest listening to music before medical procedures to help their patients relax.
>
> In the classroom, consider playing calming music after a transition or at the beginning or end of an instructional activity. You can also combine calming music with breathing exercises and other relaxation techniques like those suggested in the action strategies.
>
> Another option is to play lively music when it's a dreary day. Some of the action strategies explain easy-to-use movement activities, all of which can be done to music.
>
> Experiment with a variety of music genres and artists and ask students how specific songs make them feel. You can also give students opportunities to request or suggest music they enjoy and create a playlist.

Many children and adolescents do not have access to these kinds of anxiety intervention programs at school, much less individual or group counseling opportunities. Some of the barriers to treatment are a lack of qualified personnel to provide interventions, costs associated with implementation, not enough time to devote to the program, and school leadership teams and specialists who lack awareness that childhood anxiety is a critical mental health issue that can be addressed through school-based programs.

And yet, teachers are the first line of intervention for students with anxiety and other mental health disorders—even when they have little or no training, materials, time, or supervised support. Behavior analyst and special educator Jessica Minahan (2019) strongly supports efforts to educate teachers and give them the tools needed to intervene effectively: "It's not realistic to send every anxious child to the counselor or psychologist, or to do so every time they seemed stressed out." Teachers encounter students' anxieties daily, and if they know the key strategies and principles of support, they can support students effectively.

Teachers' actions may be the first and best anxiety interventions that many students experience. Even without formal training in mental health best practices, teachers can use the action strategies and classroom suggestions found throughout this book. They can readily integrate the strategies into instruction, activities, and social experiences. Many teachers already have experience teaching and facilitating positive social interactions, helping students learn to recognize and manage emotional stressors, and teaching students the skills needed to regulate their behavior.

Even though teachers may not be the educational professionals charged with counseling, therapeutic groups, or specific mental health programs, they can still intervene in the classroom, promote research-based practices, and positively impact anxiety-related behaviors. Through these endeavors, teachers can prevent more serious anxiety issues from developing, and they can help students develop and maintain positive coping skills that are the foundation for dealing with future stressors.

Social and Emotional Learning

The Collaborative for Academic, Social, and Emotional Learning (CASEL) explains that social and emotional learning is "the process through which all young people and adults acquire and apply the knowledge, skills, and attitudes to develop healthy identities, manage emotions and achieve personal and collective goals, feel and show empathy for others, establish and maintain supportive relationships, and make responsible and caring decisions" (2022, para. 1). These five core competencies of SEL predict children's success in school and in life.

School-based approaches to SEL are cost-effective and have a favorable impact on children's mental health and socialization. In fact, some studies have found that students' prosocial behaviors in the classroom (such as cooperating, helping, sharing, and consoling) are effective at reducing mental health difficulties, and this in turn predicts higher academic achievement (Panayiotou, Humphrey, and Wigelsworth 2019). Moreover, children's development of social and emotional skills affords them adaptive abilities to cope with stressful life events that last well into adolescence. One meta-analysis of 213 SEL studies involving 270,034 students from kindergarten through high school found that when "compared to controls, students demonstrated enhanced SEL skills, attitudes, and positive social behaviors following intervention, and demonstrated fewer conduct problems and had lower levels of emotional distress. Especially noteworthy from an educational policy perspective, academic performance was significantly improved" (Durlak et al. 2011, 405). In short, teaching social and emotional skills to children and adolescents delivers encouraging and well-substantiated results. Moreover, there is strong evidence to show that teachers are capable of teaching social and emotional skills through programs that integrate SEL into instruction, activities, and routines.

For SEL to be effective, however, students need a supportive learning environment—the classroom—where they can learn social and emotional skills and practice them with their peers in authentic contexts. Many factors contribute to a supportive setting, including teacher qualities, district policies, and parental and community involvement. But most notable are the social relationships students have at school.

FIVE CORE COMPETENCIES OF SEL

1. self-awareness
2. self-management
3. social awareness
4. relationship skills
5. responsible decision-making

Students who experience recurring stress or anxiety need and yearn for supportive relationships with teachers and peers. Without strong adult-student relationships, the trust children need so they can learn social and emotional skills will be difficult to achieve. Without strong student-student relationships, children will have difficulty practicing social skills and changing adverse thinking patterns and social habits. School can be a challenging environment for children, both academically and socially. Having close, affirming social ties can help them deal with emotional setbacks through support, encouragement, and positive feedback.

Like students, teachers experience significant stressors every day. Since the beginning of the COVID pandemic, they have been tasked with unprecedented and excessive responsibilities. Many teachers were confined at home with their own children while virtually teaching their classes. Many lacked the technology (broadband access, state-of-the-art computers, digital cameras, and Wi-Fi) and the training they needed to make online learning engaging. They also had to deal with COVID restrictions and infections in their own families. Face-to-face instruction has returned to schools, but COVID is still present in communities. All of this may cause teachers a great deal of stress and anxiety, which can affect their teaching. Indeed, their well-being impacts how they deal with difficulties in the classroom, create and maintain positive learning environments, and help regulate their students' heightened emotions. One study found that teacher stress at school not only had an impact on students' feelings and emotions, it increased their physiological stress as measured by cortisol levels too (Oberle and Schonert-Reichl 2016). The term *stress contagion* describes the phenomenon of stress spreading from one person to others.

Teachers who are dealing with post-COVID burnout may find self-care strategies such as daily exercise, healthy eating, journaling, and meditation helpful. Additionally, school leadership support for teachers (administrators who are understanding and patient with faculty) is a powerful antidote to burnout. So is professional development in participatory learning, relevant and effective materials, and classroom management. Research confirms that when teachers receive training in managing children's behavior and emotions and creating positive learning environments, their students' academic achievement improves (Jennings and Greenberg 2009).

To reflect on the information in this chapter, use the "Here's What. So What? Now What?" form on the next page to decide what key information you learned, what it means to you, and how you will implement it in your classroom and your school.

Here's What. So What? Now What?

Here's what. →

What did you learn about interventions for anxiety in children and adolescents, especially school-based interventions?

So what? →

What does this information mean to you, your students, and your learning community?

Now what? →

What can you do with this information? What changes in practice will you make?

Part 2: Twenty-Five Action Strategies to Prevent and Reduce Anxiety

CHAPTER 5

Action Strategies Explained

School-based interventions are critical for anxious students. A variety of interventions and programs can address childhood anxiety. Some include components of cognitive behavioral therapy (CBT), a psychological therapy that's particularly beneficial for anxious children. In addition, social and emotional learning (SEL) in classrooms improves children's mental health, socialization, academic achievement, and ability to cope with stressful life events. Because SEL is common in schools, many teachers already know how to foster positive social interactions, help students recognize and manage emotional stressors, and teach students how to regulate their behavior. Teachers' actions may in fact be the first and best anxiety interventions for many students.

The action strategies in this section of the book are interventions that support students with anxiety-related behaviors. Teachers can readily integrate the action strategies into instruction, activities, and social experiences. This chapter introduces the main components of the action strategies and follows with suggestions for how to select and use them.

The action strategies are appropriate for any students who demonstrate behaviors that indicate anxiety, regardless of whether the students have a diagnosed anxiety disorder. It is important to intervene as early as possible, not only to decrease the impact of anxiety and teach students how to cope with it, but also to prevent more serious mental health issues from developing. Early intervention can have a significant preventive impact.

The Action Strategies Components

Each action strategy is made up of these four elements:

1. which of the four domains the strategy addresses

2. the instructional arrangements that work for the intervention

3. which CBT component(s) the action strategy includes

4. a ready-set-go delivery model

The Four Domains

Let's review the four domains with an eye to how the action strategies align with each domain. Take a moment to glance at the Action Strategies Matrix on page 58 and note the icons associated with the domains.

Domain 1: Physiological Issues Related to Anxiety

 Many students with anxiety become so physically distressed that issues in the other domains are difficult to address. After all, it's hard to stop and think when you are you are in fight, flight, freeze, or fawn mode. Because physical distress can impair the cognitive processes associated with logic and reason (and other executive functioning skills), the first step for many teachers is to address the physiological impact of anxiety. When your priority is to help students identify and manage their emotions, recognize emotions in others, and socially engage with others after becoming upset, consider the action strategies in the physiological domain first.

The physiological manifestations of anxiety include:

- headache

- shortness of breath

- rapid heartbeat

- dry mouth

- sweaty palms

- flushed face and neck

- panic or fear

- stomachache

Many of the action strategies that address the physiological domain focus on helping students calm down. Actions such as measured deep breathing, mindfulness, and physical exercise are effective ways to get the body under control. Once these strategies have improved a student's physiological state, you can address the effects of anxiety in the behavioral, social and emotional, and academic or cognitive domains.

> **THINK ABOUT IT**
> Think about these questions as you start reading the chapter:
>
> - How will you choose which action strategies to use first?
>
> - What are your priorities? Will you consider specific students, common issues in the classroom, or strategies that are easy to use and will give you some momentum?
>
> - How can whole-class strategies support all your students? When considering your whole class, what needs are greatest?
>
> - How will you decide when to ask for additional support from a counselor, psychologist, behavior specialist, or social worker?

Domain 2: Behavioral Issues Related to Anxiety

It can be tricky to figure out what causes students' behaviors. Sometimes anxiety-related behaviors resemble mental health conditions, such as attention deficit hyperactivity disorder (ADHD) (for example, students may constantly fidget, be unable to concentrate on tasks, or act without thinking) or oppositional defiant disorder (ODD) (for instance, they might refuse to obey authority figures, be aggressive to their peers, or run away). Other times, students with anxiety may have additional mental health conditions such as depression or conduct disorder. Some students with anxiety are quiet, shy, and withdrawn, while others may exhibit the following behaviors:

- motor restlessness

- fidgeting

- problems concentrating

- perfectionism

- defensiveness

- sensitivity

The action strategies that address the behavioral domain focus on these behaviors and recognize that students with anxiety—like all students—function more effectively in the classroom when they have affirming, trusting relationships with teachers. A relationship with a caring adult can make a significant difference in a student's life. To help students improve their abilities to self-regulate, that relationship needs to provide opportunities for calm interactions in response to emotional distress and dialogue about the students' feelings. Because these action strategies are designed as positive behavioral interventions that prevent emotionally harmful behavior through proactive support, they benefit all students—not just those with anxiety.

Domain 3: Social and Emotional Issues Related to Anxiety

Without a healthy emotional state and prosocial skills, students are unlikely to do well academically. In addition, teachers may find themselves attending to many behavioral problems in classrooms and common areas. *All* students can benefit from school-based social and emotional learning initiatives. Some of the most common social and emotional difficulties demonstrated by anxious students are:

- reluctance or unwillingness to engage in new situations or to enter new settings

- withdrawal from situations, especially new ones

- shyness, especially around strangers

- lack of eye contact

- fearfulness, especially with new or varied situations or people

- lack of interest in exploring or getting to know unfamiliar people, places, or things

The action strategies that address the social and emotional domain focus on supporting students as they increase their number of social interactions with others, including participating in classroom activities. Because time spent in school is not just instructional time in the classroom, school staff should also address social and emotional issues in nonacademic settings. For younger students, these settings include the cafeteria, hallways, playground, buses, and other common areas. Older students may need support in similar environments within the school: in the hallways and cafeteria, at pep rallies or sports events, at social events such as dances, in clubs or after-school activities, and on the bus. The action strategies that address this domain can be a good first step, but many students will need ample encouragement and practice to improve their social skills.

Domain 4: Academic or Cognitive Issues Related to Anxiety

 In the past, educators may not have recognized the relationships among academic performance, cognitive functioning, and anxiety. Nevertheless, these three are closely connected.

While an academic issue, such as failing to complete independent work, may be caused by a learning disability, a lack of understanding, or an opposition to being told what to do, it's important to remember that anxiety might be a cause. For example, a student with anxiety may fail to complete an assignment because they are so perfectionistic that they rip up their first five attempts. An intervention that takes the student's anxiety into consideration is more likely to be effective than a general intervention focused on work completion.

Anxiety can also cause cognitive issues, especially related to executive functioning. Planning, problem-solving, organization, and other high-level skills may be difficult when anxiety interferes with a student's thinking process. The action strategies that address the academic or cognitive domain give you practical tools to overcome these anxiety-related obstacles:

- **Preoccupation with something or someone:** A student obsesses, or thinks constantly, about a specific issue or person and as a result, can hardly focus on matters at hand.

- **Excessive worrying about performance or achievement:** Students' anxiety can manifest with repeated thoughts over their ability to perform a task, whether it's playing a solo in a concert or competing in a sports meet. The excessive worry can be based on a fear of failing, being humiliated, or experiencing rejection.

- **Perfectionism:** Students may strive to produce flawless work and to control situations and peers. They may be overly critical of themselves and others and may have unrealistic standards.

- **Lack of participation with peers in academic and nonacademic settings:** Students avoid socializing with their peers. They isolate themselves when social opportunities are available or they withdraw during collaborative learning activities.

- **Lack of concentration:** Students may have difficulty focusing in class, sitting still, thinking clearly, or finishing classwork. Students may often lose critical materials such as textbooks, papers, pencils, or worksheets.

- **Failure to develop or articulate a plan:** Students need help creating and managing a plan (such as an outline, a checklist, or a calendar-based planner) to set and achieve desired goals.

- **Memory impairment:** Even though students can often remember things well, when they are anxious, their memory can be impaired.

Take a moment to review the table that follows, which provides a list of anxiety-related behaviors associated with each domain. Consider these behaviors as signs that a student may be experiencing anxiety. Then select and use any action strategies listed alongside the behavior indicators to support the student. The next section explains implementation steps.

Behavioral Indicators and Strategies to Address Them

Domain	If You Observe These Behaviors	Try These Strategies	
Physiological	■ headache ■ shortness of breath ■ rapid heartbeat ■ dry mouth ■ sweaty palms ■ flushed face and neck ■ panic or fear ■ stomachache	1: Track Anxiety Using a Calendar 2: Check Myself 4: Deep Breathing Exercises 5: Visualization Countdown 7: Thanks for Three 8: Go, Move, Focus 9: Positive Pictures for Positive Feelings 10: Everyone Move!	11: School Thanks 12: The Calm-Down Menu 13: Coping Toolbox 14: A Team of Friends 15: Box of Worries 16: Gratitude Journal 19: Check-Ins That Work 22: De-Stress Your Directions 25: Secret Signals
Behavioral	■ motor restlessness ■ fidgeting ■ problems concentrating ■ perfectionism ■ defensiveness ■ sensitivity	3: What Not to Think 5: Visualization Countdown 6: My Worry Plan 10: Everyone Move! 11: School Thanks 12: The Calm-Down Menu 13: Coping Toolbox 14: A Team of Friends 15: Box of Worries 17: Yet and Right Now	18: Working in Twos 19: Check-Ins That Work 20: Visual Cue Cards 21: Visual Scheduling 22: De-Stress Your Directions 23: Previews 24: Step-by-Step Project Planners 25: Secret Signals
Social and emotional	■ reluctance or unwillingness to engage in new situations or to enter new settings ■ withdrawal from situations, especially new ones ■ shyness, especially around strangers ■ lack of eye contact ■ fearfulness, especially with new or varied situations or people ■ lack of interest in exploring or getting to know unfamiliar people, places, or things	1: Track Anxiety Using a Calendar 2: Check Myself 3: What Not to Think 4: Deep Breathing Exercises 5: Visualization Countdown 6: My Worry Plan 7: Thanks for Three 8: Go, Move, Focus 9: Positive Pictures for Positive Feelings 10: Everyone Move! 11: School Thanks	12: The Calm-Down Menu 13: Coping Toolbox 14: A Team of Friends 15: Box of Worries 16: Gratitude Journal 17: Yet and Right Now 18: Working in Twos 19: Check-Ins That Work 22: De-Stress Your Directions 25: Secret Signals
Academic or cognitive	■ preoccupation with something or someone ■ excessive worrying about performance or achievement ■ perfectionism ■ lack of participation with peers in academic and nonacademic settings ■ lack of concentration ■ failure to develop or articulate a plan ■ memory impairment	3: What Not to Think 5: Visualization Countdown 6: My Worry Plan 7: Thanks for Three 10: Everyone Move! 11: School Thanks 12: The Calm-Down Menu 14: A Team of Friends 15: Box of Worries 17: Yet and Right Now	18: Working in Twos 19: Check-Ins That Work 20: Visual Cue Cards 21: Visual Scheduling 22: De-Stress Your Directions 23: Previews 24: Step-by-Step Project Planners 25: Secret Signals

Keep in mind that students' anxiety may present through a range of behaviors in more than one domain. Think about the domains that are involved when a student who is extremely withdrawn begins to self-isolate and refuses to participate in small-group activities in the classroom. Later, when their refusal escalates to defiance, they get so agitated that they become sick to their stomach. Notice how the social and emotional, behavioral, and physiological domains manifest in the student's behaviors. It may be hard for the teacher to determine which issue came first, which is most concerning, and which domain should be addressed right away. Most importantly, the teacher must approach the student in a supportive and caring manner.

Instructional Arrangements

The action strategies with the whole-group icon can help all students develop skills to cope with anxiety. The instruction and activities complement school-wide curricula that are focused on students' mental health and benefit children whose anxiety is harder to recognize.

The action strategies with the small-group icon are intended for a cluster of students who share similar issues. These strategies are both preventive and interventional.

The action strategies with the individual icon are best implemented in a private setting by a teacher, counselor, social worker, or school psychologist. These activities aim to support students who have said they are anxious or are considered anxious by teachers and need help.

CBT Components

Some of the action strategies include CBT components. The CBT icon indicates that a strategy contains one or more components of CBT.

Ready-Set-Go

Ready-set-go is a three-step method for implementing each action strategy. The "ready" step is an introduction that answers the fundamental question, *Why is this strategy important?* It also provides key background information. This information can help you determine whether the strategy is appropriate to implement with specific students.

The "set" step helps you prepare to teach the strategy. It tells you what you should know and do before you gather the student(s) and start teaching. Sometimes this step helps you understand and communicate a concept related to anxiety; sometimes it describes the materials you will need; sometimes it does both. This support is essential for busy teachers whose time for additional lesson planning is limited.

The "go" step tells you what to say and do with your students. Read this step ahead of time and adapt the procedures to meet your unique needs. Feel free to individualize all items of discussions, forms, and other resources to suit your students.

The Action Strategies Matrix

Action Strategy Instructional Arrangements	Physiological Domain	Behavioral Domain	Social and Emotional Domain	Academic or Cognitive Domain
1: Track Anxiety Using a Calendar small group individual	✓		✓	
2: Check Myself whole group small group individual	✓		✓	
3: What Not to Think whole group small group individual		✓	✓	✓
4: Deep Breathing Exercises whole group small group individual	✓		✓	
5: Visualization Countdown whole group small group individual	✓	✓	✓	✓
6: My Worry Plan small group individual		✓	✓	
7: Thanks for Three whole group small group individual	✓		✓	✓
8: Go, Move, Focus whole group small group	✓		✓	
9: Positive Pictures for Positive Feelings whole group small group individual	✓		✓	

CONTINUED ➡

Action Strategy Instructional Arrangements	Physiological Domain	Behavioral Domain	Social and Emotional Domain	Academic or Cognitive Domain
10: Everyone Move! whole group small group individual	✓	✓	✓	✓
11: School Thanks whole group small group individual	✓	✓	✓	✓
12: The Calm-Down Menu whole group small group individual	✓	✓	✓	✓
13: Coping Toolbox whole group small group individual	✓	✓	✓	
14: A Team of Friends whole group small group	✓	✓	✓	✓
15: Box of Worries whole group small group individual	✓	✓	✓	✓
16: Gratitude Journal whole group small group individual	✓		✓	
17: Yet and Right Now whole group small group individual		✓	✓	✓
18: Working in Twos whole group small group		✓	✓	✓
19: Check-Ins That Work whole group small group individual	✓	✓	✓	✓

CONTINUED ➡

← CONTINUED

Action Strategy Instructional Arrangements	Physiological Domain	Behavioral Domain	Social and Emotional Domain	Academic or Cognitive Domain
20: Visual Cue Cards individual		✓		✓
21: Visual Scheduling whole group small group individual		✓		✓
22: De-Stress Your Directions whole group small group	✓	✓	✓	✓
23: Previews whole group small group individual		✓		✓
24: Step-by-Step Project Planners whole group small group individual		✓		✓
25: Secret Signals individual	✓	✓	✓	✓

How to Use the Action Strategies

When you are concerned about student behaviors, we recommend that you approach the student positively and calmly—smile, greet them using their name, pat them on the shoulder; use a soft voice and friendly tone, choose a private, comfortable setting to talk, use encouraging phrases. Start with a friendly conversation:

- Ask how things are going.
- Tell the student you care about them and they are important to you.
- Tell them your concerns honestly. Explain that you don't want them to get hurt, and you want them to have positive experiences.
- Remind them that your job as a teacher is to guide them.
- Tell them you're going to keep tabs on how they behave in the classroom.
- Ask them to keep in touch with you.

Also, gather information from the student's parents, caregivers, and other teachers. It may not be possible to gather all the information you would like to have. When students do not have close relationships with others (especially adults), have experienced trauma, or have moved and changed schools often or are in other challenging situations, finding someone who can answer the following questions may be difficult. Try to gather as much information as possible, so interventions have a greater chance of being effective. Consider asking:

- How does the student control their emotional responses?
- How does the student self-soothe and/or calm down?
- What difficulties does the student encounter with self-soothing and/or calming down?
- What difficulties does the student exhibit in controlling their emotions?
- How does the student express worry, fear, or anger?
- How would you describe the student's emotions, behaviors, and sense of connection to others when stressed?
- How often does the student become agitated or dysregulated to the point of social and academic difficulty?
- How does the student reengage with others after becoming upset?
- What dangerous behaviors does the student exhibit when stressed?
- When does the student have temper tantrums; fight, flight, freeze, or fawn reactions; and reduced ability to plan, organize, and commit to tasks?
- How often does the student cry, stress out, daydream, or complain of muscle tension, fatigue, headaches, stomachaches, or other physical discomforts?
- How would you describe the student's social skills with peers?

Before selecting action strategies, gather with a small team of school professionals who have knowledge of the student and/or who interact with them. This group may include the student's teacher(s), counselor, social worker, and school psychologist. It might be the school intervention team, a grade-level team, or a support team. Invite the school nurse to join the team if the student takes medication for anxiety and invite a learning specialist who has expertise in academic issues, if such a specialist is available.

At the team meeting, use the preceding questions and reports from meetings with the student and their caregivers to decide which behaviors are of immediate concern. The team can use the following questions to identify instances when anxiety seems to increase in the student:

- What anxious behaviors were observed?
- What were the circumstances in which the anxious behaviors were observed?
- What was the setting in which the anxious behaviors were observed?
- What happened before, during, and after the anxiety was observed?
- Who was there?
- Was there a precipitating event? If so, what was it?
- Is a pattern visible? What is the pattern?

At the team meeting, select action strategies to try. Deciding which behavior or issue to address first will depend on the team's assessment of the student's current functioning, history, and responsiveness to interventions. Consider any or all of these factors:

- the most noticeable issue that is affecting the student's mental health and well-being
- the issue that has the most significant impact on the student's learning
- a behavior pattern that is escalating (for example, crying in class more often or becoming more withdrawn throughout the school day)
- behaviors that interfere with the student's relationships, resulting in isolation or loneliness
- an issue that disrupts teaching and other students' learning
- a priority identified by an IEP or by special education or discipline/behavioral intervention committees

After deciding on one or two action strategies, the teacher, counselor, or team should commit to faithful application of the intervention. Keep in mind that the strategy or strategies may not work. Each student is an individual and will respond uniquely. If an intervention does not have a positive impact after a reasonable amount of time, move on to another intervention and make a commitment to implementing it for a reasonable amount of time. Continue to problem-solve and maintain a positive attitude.

REMINDER
Remember that students with a diagnosed anxiety disorder who have an individualized education program (IEP) should always be taught within the legally prescribed framework of special education services. Communication with parents or caregivers and the student's general practice physician and/or psychiatrist is critical and required by law.

Track Anxiety Using a Calendar

DOMAINS ADDRESSED	INSTRUCTION	CBT COMPONENT
social and emotional	small group	self-monitoring
physiological	individual	

Ready

Two important steps for students learning to deal with their anxiety are recognizing when they are feeling anxious and describing what it feels like. You can help students identify when anxiety appears by using a calendar-based document or tool. After two weeks or so, you and each student can look for patterns of events, situations, stressors, people, or types of thinking that trigger their anxiety. Then you can develop a plan to help reduce the students' anxiety using selected action strategies.

Set

Review the characteristics of anxiety described in chapter 1 so you can explain it in ways that are developmentally appropriate based on your students' ages, levels of understanding, and prior exposure to information about anxiety. Use simple, clear explanations of what anxiety is and how it affects people. Here's one definition, adapted from the Centers for Disease Control and Prevention (CDC) and National Health Service Scotland, that students of various ages may understand:

> Anxiety is an uncomfortable feeling. It can feel like worry, nervousness, or fear. People often feel anxious when change is happening or when something is stressful. You may feel afraid when you are anxious, but you may also feel angry or be tired or have a headache or an upset stomach.

Review Action Strategy 2: Check Myself. It focuses on self-awareness too. You can pair it with this strategy to spark a discussion about what anxiety is, what can cause it, and how it feels. Ask students to complete a Check Myself card identifying the specific feelings and reactions they have when they feel anxious.

Go

1. Give each student a daily, weekly, or monthly calendar to fill in. This can be a standard paper calendar or journal, an online version, or an app. For young students, nonreaders, and English learners, use the How I Feel Daily Journal on page 66. For older students, use the Two-Week Calendar on page 67.

2. After reviewing the characteristics of anxiety (see chapter 1) and some of the feelings associated with it (see Action Strategy 2: Check Myself), explain to your students that they will be focusing on times when they feel anxious. Mention that they will keep entries on a calendar to help them identify patterns of events, situations, stressors, people, or types of thinking that happen when they feel anxious.

3. For younger students, write the subject areas in the first column of the How I Feel chart. Read aloud the name of each subject, then ask the student to circle the face that matches how they feel. Then encourage them to choose a number from the list of reasons or draw a picture that explains the reason for their feelings. Review and discuss orally. Keep tracking students' anxiety for up to two weeks.

4. When you're working with older students, tell them to describe the feelings that come along with anxiety on the day and time it appears. As the students write their entries, they should reflect on these questions:

   ■ When (day, time, class period) did you experience anxiety?

   ■ What happened at the same time?

   ■ What did you experience?

   ■ How did you feel physically?

   Older students can also note how long the anxiety lasted, where they were in the setting (for example, in a group activity, approaching a circle of peers, alone in a band practice room), who they were with, and what the demands of the situation were. They can write feelings associated with worry, nervousness, stress, and fear, such as *I couldn't concentrate, I froze and didn't want to speak, I kept thinking that I was going to say the wrong answer*, or *I got super sad*. These feelings can be coupled with physical complaints. For example, *I couldn't catch my breath, I started to sweat*, or *My stomach hurt*.

   Advise older students to keep tracking their anxiety episodes for two weeks so they can later determine how often these episodes occur, how long they last, in what settings they develop, and other associated factors (for example, how severe they are or how their peers or adults responded).

5. After tracking students' anxiety for several days, you, a counselor, or an intervention team can meet privately with individual students, carefully review each student's calendar entries, discuss the feelings and physical complaints they noted, and identify patterns (for example, *I noticed that I am most worried in math, when I have to solve problems in front of others or share my work publicly*).

6. Next, develop a plan to help reduce a student's anxiety so they can function in school with less stress. Invite the student to participate in developing the plan, allowing them to choose the action strategies they want to try.

Two-Week Calendar

Name: Rochelle

Date: March 14–25

Keep these questions in mind as you write your daily entries:
- When (day, time, class period) did you experience anxiety?
- What happened at the same time?
- What did you experience?
- How did you feel physically?

Monday Date: March 14	Tuesday Date: March 15	Wednesday Date: March 16	Thursday Date: March 17	Friday Date: March 18
Math I was called on to read a problem. I felt embarrassed because I thought I'd get the problem wrong in front of everybody. I could feel my face get red. I got warm.	Lunch No one invited me to sit with them. I could not think straight. I thought everyone was thinking what a loser I am. I started to shake.	Math I had to work a problem on the whiteboard. I knew the answer but got mixed up. I could not explain it. I started to mumble. My stomach started to hurt. I wanted to throw up.		Math I got sweaty and nervous as soon as I entered the room. I was dreading working in groups. I didn't speak at all. I worried the entire time I was in class. I was just scared.
Monday Date: March 21	Tuesday Date: March 22	Wednesday Date: March 23	Thursday Date: March 24	Friday Date: March 25
All morning long I did not want to come to school today. My stomach hurt. I didn't eat breakfast or lunch.	Lunch No one asks me to sit with them. I'm scared the whole time. I want to run away. My palms are sweaty. My heart is racing. I feel like I want to throw up.	Math I had to work a problem on the whiteboard. I knew the answer but got mixed up. I could not explain it. I started to mumble. My stomach started to hurt. I wanted to throw up.	Lunch No one asks me to sit with them. I'm scared the whole time. I want to run away. My palms are sweaty. My heart is racing. I feel like I want to throw up.	

Help Anxious Kids in a Stressful World © David Campos and Kathleen McConnell Fad—Free Spirit Publishing

67

How I Feel Daily Journal

Name _____   **Date** _____

Subject	How I Feel	Why I Feel This Way
	😊 😐 😞	
	😊 😐 😞	
	😊 😐 😞	
	😊 😐 😞	
	😊 😐 😞	
	😊 😐 😞	
	😊 😐 😞	

Reason Key

1. I miss someone special to me.

2. Someone is being mean to me. 😠

3. I'm afraid. 😢

4. The work is too hard.

5. (Draw your own reason.)

Help Anxious Kids in a Stressful World © David Campos and Kathleen McConnell Fad—Free Spirit Publishing

Two-Week Calendar

Name _____ Date _____

Keep these questions in mind as you write your daily entries:
- When (day, time, class period) did you experience anxiety?
- What happened at the same time?
- What did you experience?
- How did you feel physically?

Monday Date:	Tuesday Date:	Wednesday Date:	Thursday Date:	Friday Date:
Monday Date:	Tuesday Date:	Wednesday Date:	Thursday Date:	Friday Date:

Check Myself

DOMAINS ADDRESSED	INSTRUCTION	CBT COMPONENT
physiological	whole group	self-monitoring
social and emotional	small group	
	individual	

Ready

Children and adolescents often have trouble realizing when their anxiety is intensifying. Many times they have not been taught to recognize and tune in to the physical and emotional signs of anxiety. In addition, when their anxiety is heightened, it can be difficult for them to recognize and process how anxious they really are. If children don't realize they are getting anxious, they may behave in ways that impede their learning or relationships. After discussing what anxiety is and how it can look, students can use the Check Myself activity sheet to identify their own anxious feelings and strategies they could use to reduce those feelings.

Set

Take a moment to review the characteristics of anxiety explained in chapter 1. Then prepare a definition of anxiety that is developmentally appropriate for your students. A simple, clear definition with examples suited for your grade level and school community works best. A guided discussion of how anxiety presents emotionally and physically follows. Review the five discussion prompts (step 2 under "Go") and take some time to consider how you might adapt them for your students, circumstances, and climate. Consider recording students' ideas on the board or on an anchor chart so they can refer to them while completing their Check Myself forms.

Go

1. Explain what anxiety is using a simple definition that is age-appropriate and suitable for your students' knowledge and understanding. For example, to a group of third graders you might say, "Anxiety is being very worried about or afraid of something. Everyone feels anxious sometimes, which is normal. But if we start to worry and fear

too often, we might behave in ways that harm us. It's important to recognize anxious feelings so we can deal with them before they stress us out or hurt our relationships."

2. Discuss anxiety with your students using these questions as prompts. Record the students' answers on the board or chart paper.

   - What makes you anxious at school? At home? Out in the community?

   - When do you feel the most anxious?

   - How do you know that you are anxious?

   - What emotions do you feel when you are anxious? (With younger children, explain that anxiety feels like sadness and fear.)

   - How do you feel physically when you are anxious? (Prompt younger children to recognize body sensations like stomachaches, headaches, and shakiness.)

3. Invite your students to generate a list of three to seven signs of anxiety they can check themselves for. Their responses might include:

   - I can't make eye contact with anyone.

   - My mouth gets dry.

   - My heart starts racing.

   - I start breathing hard.

   - I feel like I can't breathe.

   - I start shaking.

   - My stomach hurts.

   - I want to throw up.

   - I want to cry.

   - My face gets red.

   - I feel hot.

   - I keep thinking of the same thing over and over.

4. Provide each student with an age-appropriate Check Myself activity sheet. (For younger children or nonreaders, use Check Myself: Am I Worried or Afraid? on page 71. For older students, use Check Myself: Signs of Anxiety on page 72.) Encourage the students to answer the questions and fill in the blank spaces. With younger students, complete the forms together while reading them out loud. Students can keep their completed forms in a notebook or anywhere else that's both handy and private. Students may wish to add to or redo their forms later, as they learn more about anxiety and themselves.

5. Review and teach strategies that aim to reduce anxiety. These could be strategies you already know and use or action strategies from this book. Older students can write the strategies they plan to use to reduce their anxiety. With younger students or

nonreaders, brainstorm strategies that might help them. In the meantime, you can give them some quick tips to manage their anxiety, such as taking three deep breaths, counting to ten slowly, asking the teacher for a quick break, thinking of something funny, finding something positive in the situation, or asking the teacher for a few minutes to talk to a friend about the anxiety they are feeling.

Check Myself: Signs of Anxiety

Name Taylor   Date October 6

I can check myself to help with my anxiety. I know I am anxious when I notice these signs:

I feel my face and neck get hot.

I feel my heart beating very fast.

I can't seem to remember anything.

When I notice these signs, I can reduce my anxiety by:

Counting slowly to ten and then taking three deep breaths. If I really need a break, I'll ask my teacher if I can have a drink of water.

Help Anxious Kids in a Stressful World © David Campos and Kathleen McConnell Fad · Free Spirit Publishing

73

Check Myself: Am I Worried or Afraid?

Name _____ **Date** _____

Are you worried or afraid? Circle your answer: yes   no

How do you feel right now? Circle your answer:

happy   meh   sad   anxious   scared

Do you need help? Circle your answer: yes   no

Tell me what might help you: _____

Or draw a picture of what might help you:

Check Myself: Signs of Anxiety

Name _____ **Date** _____

I can check myself to help with my anxiety. I know I am anxious when I notice these signs:

_____

_____

_____

_____

_____

When I notice these signs, I can reduce my anxiety by:

_____

_____

_____

_____

_____

_____

Help Anxious Kids in a Stressful World © David Campos and Kathleen McConnell Fad—Free Spirit Publishing

ACTION STRATEGY 3

What Not to Think

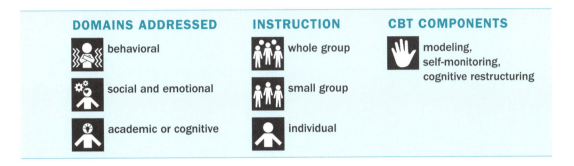

DOMAINS ADDRESSED	INSTRUCTION	CBT COMPONENTS
behavioral	whole group	modeling, self-monitoring, cognitive restructuring
social and emotional	small group	
academic or cognitive	individual	

Ready

Anxious students often engage in negative thinking patterns that intensify their anxiety. These negative thoughts can lead to words and actions that are emotionally harmful and unproductive. This action strategy aims to help students recognize ways of thinking that exacerbate their anxiety and adversely affect their behavior, then replace their negative thought patterns with positive thoughts and affirmations.

Set

Review the characteristics of anxiety in chapter 1 and read the section in chapter 2 titled Across the Lifespan (page 24) for background information on typical fears and worries at various developmental stages. Familiarize yourself with the types of anxious thinking summarized in the following table.

Type of Anxious Thinking	What It Means	Examples
Catastrophizing	Worrying that the worst possible outcome is going to happen	■ No one at my new school is going to like me. I bet they'll beat me up. ■ My mom is late picking me up. She could be dead. ■ Someone might kidnap me if I walk home from school.
All or nothing	Viewing situations as all good or all bad (black or white), with no nuance	■ I have the worst family in the whole wide world. We fight all the time. ■ The teacher said to study for half an hour, but I only had fifteen minutes. So I didn't bother studying at all. ■ I thought Ms. Jones was going to be a fun teacher, but all teachers are awful.

CONTINUED ➡

← CONTINUED

Type of Anxious Thinking	What It Means	Examples
Mind reading	Believing you know what other people are thinking—and it's usually bad	■ *The kids on the bus stare at me when I get on. They all think I'm dirty and poor.* ■ *In math, everyone knows the answers but me, and they are waiting for me to make a mistake.* ■ *I said the wrong answer in social studies and now everyone thinks I'm stupid.*
Fortune-telling	Insisting you can predict the future—and it's usually bad (related to mind reading)	■ *I bet my dad will forget to pick me up.* ■ *I almost failed science last year. I bet I will fail for sure this year.* ■ *When we get assigned to groups, I bet I'll be assigned to the loser group. I always am.*

If your students are in the early grades, keep in mind how young children make developmentally appropriate statements that demonstrate anxious thinking. They might make comments like the following:

- "No one is going to play with me at the party."
- "Everybody hates me."
- "All the kids think I'm dumb because I don't have a Barbie."
- "I know Mommy is going to get in a car crash today."

You can use all this information to help students articulate the thoughts they have when they are worried, anxious, fearful, or stressed—which are typically negative—and reframe them to be positive and affirming.

Go

1. Explain what anxiety is. A simple, age-appropriate definition suited for the students' level of knowledge and understanding works best. See the examples in action strategies 1 and 2 (pages 63 and 68, respectively).

2. Share some of the typical worries and fears that children and adolescents experience. Younger students often worry about separation from or harm to their parents. Students in the middle grades may feel anxiety over the dark, animals, and natural disasters. As students grow older, their anxiety often centers on school, performing in front of others, not fitting in, or being rejected by their peers. See the discussion in chapter 2 titled Across the Lifespan (page 24) for additional information on typical fears and worries at various developmental stages.

3. Use the information from the preceding table on pages 73–74 for a lesson on the types of anxious thinking, which are all problematic. Explain that everyone sometimes engages in negative, unproductive thinking. With younger students, explain that they may have "bad thoughts" about people, circumstances, and events. Point out that when people get into a long-term habit of harmful thinking, it negatively affects their attitudes and behavior. They may even develop physical problems.

4. Ask students to think of some examples of their own that demonstrate negative thinking patterns (bad thoughts). The types of anxious thinking overlap, so students may offer similar responses.

5. Give each student a copy of the What Not to Think chart. Have students first read the anxious thoughts printed on the What Not to Think side of the chart. (For a challenge, ask students to identify the type of thinking each sentence describes—catastrophizing, all or nothing, mind reading, or fortune-telling.) Then they can complete the What to Think Instead side of the chart. With young students, nonreaders, or English learners, read the What Not to Think thoughts and write their What to Think Instead responses for them, or invite them to draw pictures that represent their responses.

6. Later, ask students to write their own anxious thoughts and what to think instead in the blank spaces.

7. Encourage students to share what they have written. Then ask each student to choose one What to Think Instead thought they can use across varied situations. Here are some affirmations that work in a variety of circumstances:

   - *I've got this.*
   - *I can do this.*
   - *It's going to be okay.*
   - *I'm going to push through.*
   - *I can handle this.*
   - *I know how to deal with this.*
   - *This is just a blip. Keep going.*
   - *I can try again.*
   - *Nothing is forever.*
   - *Mistakes happen.*
   - *If I make a mistake, I can start over.*

8. Encourage students to use What to Think Instead affirmations whenever they feel anxiety creeping in.

What Not to Think

Name _____ **Date** _____

What Not to Think	What to Think Instead
Everyone hates me.	
I can never do anything right.	
I look ugly.	
When I get called on, I never know the answer.	
I will never understand math.	
At recess, no one ever wants to play with me.	

CONTINUED ➡

Help Anxious Kids in a Stressful World © David Campos and Kathleen McConnell Fad—Free Spirit Publishing

What Not to Think (Continued)

Name _____ **Date** _____

What Not to Think	What to Think Instead
My parents fight a lot. I know they will get divorced.	
My math teacher won't help me because she thinks I'm dumb.	
No one at my new school will ask me to eat lunch with them.	
Even though I study, I can never do well on tests.	
When I do my presentation, I know it will sound stupid.	
Last year, I always got in trouble. I know this year will be just the same.	

Help Anxious Kids in a Stressful World © David Campos and Kathleen McConnell Fad—Free Spirit Publishing

Deep Breathing Exercises

DOMAINS ADDRESSED	INSTRUCTION	CBT COMPONENTS
physiological	whole group	modeling, self-monitoring, relaxation
social and emotional	small group	
	individual	

Ready

Breathing and anxiety are closely related in humans. When people are anxious, they tend to take shallow breaths that often cause physical symptoms, which in turn make them even more anxious. Since breathing is automatic and children rarely think about it, they may not realize when their breathing changes. They also may not know that their breathing affects how they feel physically and emotionally. This strategy offers four deep breathing exercises that students can learn to use to relax and reduce their anxiety.

Set

Teach students deep breathing exercises when they are calm. They may be unable to learn the exercises when they're feeling anxious. Students can use the exercises when needed, in moments of heightened worry or tension.

This action strategy presents four deep breathing exercises: Belly Breathing, 4-4-4 Breathing, Kiss Breathing, and Blow-Out-the-Candles Breathing. Teach one exercise at a time until the students are comfortable with all of them. Model each exercise slowly and carefully. Make sure students can see you clearly, so they know when you are breathing in and out. Follow up with plenty of guided practice. Allow the students to select their favorites as needed or stick with one exercise that works best for the class.

Go

1. For each of these exercises, model how to breathe and then ask the students to practice by following your example. You can say the steps out loud as the students practice.

   ■ **Belly Breathing:**

   a. Sit on a chair or on the floor, or stand.

   b. Take a moment to relax your shoulders, arms, and legs. Shake them if it helps you loosen up your body.

   c. Place both hands on your belly.

   d. Close your eyes if you like.

   e. Breathe in through your nose and feel your belly expand.

   f. Breathe out through your mouth.

   g. Repeat several times, then open your eyes.

   ■ **4-4-4 Breathing:**

   a. Sit on a chair or on the floor, or stand.

   b. Take a moment to relax your shoulders, arms, and legs. Shake them if it helps you loosen up your body.

   c. Close your eyes if you like.

   d. Breathe in for a slow count of four.

   e. Hold for a slow count of four.

   f. Breathe out for a slow count of four.

   g. Repeat several times, then open your eyes.

   ■ **Kiss Breathing:**

   a. Sit on a chair or on the floor, or stand.

   b. Take a moment to relax your shoulders, arms, and legs. Shake them if it helps you loosen up your body.

   c. Close your eyes if you like.

   d. Breathe in through your nose with your mouth closed for a count of two.

   e. Pucker your lips like a kiss.

   f. Breathe out slowly through your mouth for a count of four.

   g. Repeat several times, then open your eyes.

   ■ **Blow-Out-the-Candles Breathing:**

   a. Sit on a chair or on the floor, or stand.

b. Take a moment to relax your shoulders, arms, and legs. Shake them if it helps you loosen up your body.

   c. Close your eyes if you like.

   d. Close your mouth and breathe in through your nose.

   e. Pretend that you are going to blow out candles on a birthday cake.

   f. Blow out your breath slowly so that you blow out all the candles.

   g. Repeat several times, then open your eyes.

2. Consider using a timer with a beeper or chime to tell your students when it's time for deep breathing exercises. For example, maybe you will do the exercises hourly. When the timer sounds, the whole class can take a few moments to do a selected deep breathing exercise.

3. After the students learn these deep breathing exercises, encourage them to practice on their own, especially when they feel anxious. On pages 81–82, you'll find cue cards you can give to students who need reminders about deep breathing.

Deep Breathing Cue Cards

Belly Breathing

1. Sit on a chair or on the floor, or stand.

2. Take a moment to relax your shoulders, arms, and legs. Shake them if it helps you loosen up your body.

3. Place both hands on your belly.

4. Close your eyes if you like.

5. Breathe in through your nose and feel your belly expand.

6. Breathe out through your mouth.

7. Repeat several times, then open your eyes.

4-4-4 Breathing

1. Sit on a chair or on the floor, or stand.

2. Take a moment to relax your shoulders, arms, and legs. Shake them if it helps you loosen up your body.

3. Close your eyes if you like.

4. Breathe in for a slow count of four.

5. Hold for a slow count of four.

6. Breathe out for a slow count of four.

7. Repeat several times, then open your eyes.

Help Anxious Kids in a Stressful World © David Campos and Kathleen McConnell Fad—Free Spirit Publishing

CONTINUED ➡

Deep Breathing Cue Cards *(Continued)*

Kiss Breathing

1. Sit on a chair or on the floor, or stand.

2. Take a moment to relax your shoulders, arms, and legs. Shake them if it helps you loosen up your body.

3. Close your eyes if you like.

4. Breathe in through your nose with your mouth closed for a count of two.

5. Pucker your lips like a kiss.

6. Breathe out slowly through your mouth for a count of four.

7. Repeat several times, then open your eyes.

Blow-Out-the-Candles Breathing

1. Sit on a chair or on the floor, or stand.

2. Take a moment to relax your shoulders, arms, and legs. Shake them if it helps you loosen up your body.

3. Close your eyes if you like.

4. Close your mouth and breathe in through your nose.

5. Pretend that you are going to blow out candles on a birthday cake.

6. Blow out your breath slowly so that you blow out all the candles.

7. Repeat several times, then open your eyes.

Visualization Countdown

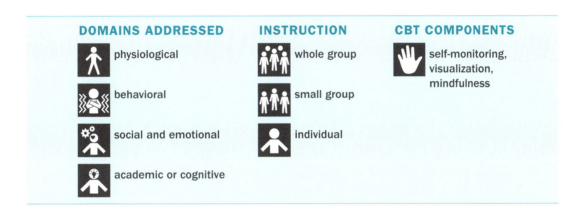

DOMAINS ADDRESSED
- physiological
- behavioral
- social and emotional
- academic or cognitive

INSTRUCTION
- whole group
- small group
- individual

CBT COMPONENTS
- self-monitoring, visualization, mindfulness

Ready

When children are anxious, they may lack focus and concentration, be easily distracted, have repetitive thoughts, and engage in negative self-talk and other destructive behaviors. These symptoms of anxiety can be problematic in the classroom, where students need to respond to questions and directions, engage in discussions, begin and complete assignments, communicate effectively with teachers and peers, and follow directions. Others may perceive anxious students as disrespectful, unengaged, lazy, defiant, or uncooperative. The good news is that you can help students clear their minds with breathing exercises that include visualizations and countdowns.

Set

Before using this strategy, review the characteristics of anxiety described in chapter 1. Action Strategies 1 and 2 also offer some ideas for how to explain anxiety and its effects simply and clearly. Next, talk about worry-based thinking, which is when the mind wanders with excessive, unpleasant thoughts that interfere with everyday functioning. To describe worry-based thinking, you can use phrases such as *you can't stop thinking about things; you worry so much, you can't do anything else; or you're stuck thinking about something.* Explain to students that you are going to teach them breathing exercises that can help them stop thinking too much (worrying) so they can focus on their schoolwork. As you teach students this strategy, expect that children will need reminders, cues, reteaching, and lots of practice.

Go

1. Ask the students to put everything away and sit quietly in their chairs or on the floor.

2. Explain to your students that they will be taking deep breaths. They can start by breathing in while counting slowly from one to three and repeating that count while breathing out.

3. After a few of these deep breathing exercises, explain to the children that as they breathe in and out, they can count down with visualizations. Tell them that visualization is noticing things or imagining things. If the students need cues, hand out the Countdown Cue Cards on pages 86–87 or project them where everyone can see them. Students can close their eyes as they do each countdown. Explain that it is no big deal if they have a hard time with the visualizations.

> ■ **Sensory Countdown**
>
> Tell your students:
>
> **a.** Imagine yourself on a beach, in the mountains, on a hiking trail, at a park, at a lake, or in some other place where you're surrounded by nature.
>
> **b.** Take a deep breath in and a deep breath out. As you breathe, think about three things you see in your imaginary place.
>
> **c.** Take another deep breath in and a deep breath out. As you breathe, think about two things you hear in your imaginary place.
>
> **d.** Take a deep breath in and another one out. As you breathe, think about one thing you smell in your imaginary place.
>
> **e.** Take a deep breath in and out. As you do, say to yourself why you appreciate the place you've imagined.

> ■ **Song-and-Dance Countdown**
>
> Tell your students:
>
> **a.** Imagine yourself on a dance floor with your family or friends.
>
> **b.** Take a deep breath in and a deep breath out. As you breathe, think about three songs you want to dance to.
>
> **c.** Take another deep breath in and a deep breath out. As you breathe, think about two dance moves you want to do.
>
> **d.** Take a deep breath in and another one out. As you breathe, think about one person you want to dance with.
>
> **e.** Take a deep breath in and out. As you do, thank the person you imagined dancing with quietly to yourself.

■ **Friendly Countdown**

Tell your students:

a. Imagine yourself with your friends.

b. Take a deep breath in and a deep breath out. As you breathe, think about three fun things you could do with your friends at school.

c. Take another deep breath in and a deep breath out. As you breathe, think about two fun things you could do with your friends at an amusement park.

d. Take a deep breath in and another one out. As you breathe, think about one fun thing you could do with your friends at a sleepover.

e. Take a deep breath in and out. As you do, thank your friends quietly to yourself.

4. Challenge your students to create their own visualization countdowns.

5. Repeat visualization countdowns with the whole class, small groups, or individual students, especially before a challenging lesson, a high-stakes test, or whenever the students seem stressed.

Countdown Cue Cards

Sensory Countdown

1. Imagine yourself on a beach, in the mountains, on a hiking trail, at a park, at a lake, or in some other place where you're surrounded by nature.

2. Take a deep breath in and a deep breath out. As you breathe, think about three things you see in your imaginary place.

3. Take another deep breath in and a deep breath out. As you breathe, think about two things you hear in your imaginary place.

4. Take a deep breath in and another one out. As you breathe, think about one thing you smell in your imaginary place.

5. Take a deep breath in and out. As you do, say to yourself why you appreciate the place you've imagined.

Song-and-Dance Countdown

1. Imagine yourself on a dance floor with your family or friends.

2. Take a deep breath in and a deep breath out. As you breathe, think about three songs you want to dance to.

3. Take another deep breath in and a deep breath out. As you breathe, think about two dance moves you want to do.

4. Take a deep breath in and another one out. As you breathe, think about one person you want to dance with.

5. Take a deep breath in and out. As you do, thank the person you imagined dancing with quietly to yourself.

Help Anxious Kids in a Stressful World © David Campos and Kathleen McConnell Fad—Free Spirit Publishing

CONTINUED ➡

Countdown Cue Cards *(Continued)*

Friendly Countdown

1. Imagine yourself with your friends.

2. Take a deep breath in and a deep breath out. As you breathe, think about three fun things you could do with your friends at school.

3. Take another deep breath in and a deep breath out. As you breathe, think about two fun things you could do with your friends at an amusement park.

4. Take a deep breath in and another one out. As you breathe, think about one fun thing you could do with your friends at a sleepover.

5. Take a deep breath in and out. As you do, thank your friends quietly to yourself.

Help Anxious Kids in a Stressful World © David Campos and Kathleen McConnell Fad—Free Spirit Publishing

My Worry Plan

DOMAINS ADDRESSED	INSTRUCTION	CBT COMPONENTS
behavioral	small group	 self-monitoring, cognitive restructuring
social and emotional	individual	

Ready

One of the key indicators of anxiety is excessive worry. When children start to worry, one worry can lead to another and worrying can get out of control. Some children may have difficulty interrupting and reducing their worrying. This strategy can help students do that by focusing on what they are worrying about and planning for to deal with their worries using specific strategies.

Set

Prepare to discuss the meaning of worry. Explain that worry is a normal human emotion. But when worries grow too big or too frequent, they can affect daily functions such as eating, sleeping, and focusing attention. This is chronic worry, which can be harmful. You might say, "Too much worry can make you feel sick (with stomachaches or headaches) and tired. It can also keep you from having fun with your family and friends or starting or finishing your schoolwork. Sometimes, too much worrying can make you feel angry at or uncomfortable around others. Teachers, counselors, and trusted adults can help you manage your worries." When students tell you they are worried, or when you observe behaviors or conversations that indicate excessive worry, use the appropriate My Worry Plan activity sheet.

Go

1. Give each student a copy of the appropriate My Worry Plan. Use My Worry Plan 1 (page 90) for younger students, nonreaders, or English learners by reading the statements out loud, encouraging students to complete as much as they can on their own, and helping them write their responses. Older students and readers can complete My Worry Plan 2 (page 91) on their own.

2. Ask the students to rate how worried they are.

3. Guide the students through the rest of the questions and prompts. Explain that there are

things they can do to reduce their worries. You might say, "Some worries may take up a lot of your time and your brain. You might worry a lot about a friend who is in the hospital, about a parent who has lost their job, or about not having good friends. There are things you can do to make those worries smaller. It helps to plan which strategies to use and when to use them."

4. Collaborate with your students to help them each identify a trusted, supportive adult who can help them come up with other strategies—from the action strategies in this book, by coming up with their own activities based on their knowledge of the student, or by engaging them in activities that distract them from their worries (such as reading to a younger group of students, helping in the library or school office, or organizing volunteer opportunities).

5. Remind students that the first strategy may not always work, so it's good to have other options.

6. After a few days, check in with students to see how they are doing and feeling and how well a strategy is working. If the first strategy does not work well, encourage students to try another one. Repeat this process if the chronic worry continues.

My Worry Plan 1

How worried are you? Circle the face that matches how you feel.

happy   meh   sad   anxious   scared

Draw what you are worried about.

How can you make this worry smaller on your own? Check as many ideas as you want. You can also add your own ideas.

❏ I can practice deep breathing exercises.

❏ I can imagine myself outside in the park, on a trail, on the beach, or in the mountains.

❏ I can imagine myself doing things with people I love.

❏ I can draw pictures of things I'm glad I have.

❏ I can call or play with friends or family.

❏ I can _____

_____

When can we talk about how you're doing? Let's choose a date:_____

Help Anxious Kids in a Stressful World © David Campos and Kathleen McConnell Fad—Free Spirit Publishing

My Worry Plan 2

Name _____ **Date** _____

How worried are you? Circle the number that matches how you feel.

1	**2**	**3**	**4**	**5**
not at all worried	not worried	not sure	a little worried	very worried

Write about or draw what is worrying you.

```
[                                                        ]
[                                                        ]
[                                                        ]
[                                                        ]
[                                                        ]
[                                                        ]
```

How can you make this worry smaller on your own? Check as many ideas as you want. You can also add your own ideas.

❏ I can practice deep breathing exercises.

❏ I can visualize myself in nature.

❏ I can visualize myself doing things with people I love.

❏ I can draw and write in my gratitude journal.

❏ I can do something nice for myself.

❏ I can call or hang out with friends or loved ones.

❏ I can draw a picture of my worries and label the emotions I have.

❏ I can _____

_____

Ask your trusted adult to check on your progress. Choose a specific date:_____

Help Anxious Kids in a Stressful World © David Campos and Kathleen McConnell Fad—Free Spirit Publishing

Thanks for Three

DOMAINS ADDRESSED	INSTRUCTION	CBT COMPONENTS
physiological	whole group	self-monitoring, cognitive restructuring
social and emotional	small group	
academic or cognitive	individual	

Ready

Thankfulness and positive thinking work together to lift students' spirits and help them recognize that goodness is often found outside themselves. Thankfulness can lead to positive thinking and vice versa. It's hard for some students to adopt and maintain a positive attitude. They may complain and feel pessimistic or anxious about school, teachers, or peers. In this strategy, students exercise a positive mindset and acknowledge their gratitude for people and good things (tangible and intangible) in their lives. Positive thinking can start small, with gratitude for modest things, and grow to a larger appreciation for health and well-being, nature, safety and security, and more.

Set

Take a moment to review the difference between positive thinking (seeing the best in life) and thankfulness (appreciating good things). Prepare a chart on a whiteboard, bulletin board, or flip chart with the headings "Positive Thinking" and "Thankfulness." Underneath the headings, write simple definitions. Think of a few examples that distinguish the two concepts, but don't write the examples yet. See the sample chart on page 94.

Have enough colored sticky notes to provide three for each student. The students will write on the sticky notes and post them onto the prepared chart for future reference. (Alternatively, give each student the activity sheets My Positive Thoughts on page 95 and My Attitude of Gratitude on page 96. You can later assemble these into a book that students can explore whenever they are struggling with their emotions, feeling sad or negative, or feeling overwhelmed.)

Go

1. Discuss what it means to think positive (being pleasant, encouraging, or hopeful; having a good outlook about people and situations). Distinguish this from thankfulness (being happy, pleased, or relieved to have something or about something that has happened).

2. Write on the chart a few examples from your own life that distinguish positive thinking from thankfulness. Your example for the former might be *It's a beautiful, sunny day. I have such great friends. I love my dog.* For the latter, *I'm glad I get to teach such great students. I appreciate my parents because they are supportive. I'm grateful for my children because they bring me joy.*

3. Say to your students: "Reflect on the day so far. What are some things to think positive about? What are some things to be thankful for?"

4. Give the students three sticky notes each. Have them number the notes as 1, 2, and 3.

5. Challenge the students to write a simple word or phrase on each sticky note as an example of positive thinking or thankfulness. For example, a student might write *great breakfast* as an example of positive thinking and *new pencil* as an example of thankfulness. Students could also draw their ideas instead of writing words.

6. After they are finished writing or drawing, pair up the students and ask the partners to share their examples with each other.

7. Invite the students to post their sticky notes onto the prepared chart. (See the sample chart on page 94.) Encourage students to add more notes later as they think of more examples. Whenever the mood in class sounds or feels negative, read some of the notes out loud. Alternatively, students can each select a note to take to their desk and reflect on similar ideas in their own lives.

8. Extend this strategy by encouraging students to share their positive and thankful thoughts with peers in other classes, their families, and school personnel.

9. As an alternative, make copies of the activity sheets My Positive Thoughts on page 95 and My Attitude of Gratitude on page 96. Explain that the word *gratitude* means "thankfulness" and *grateful* means "thankful." Ask the students to keep records of their positive thinking and gratitude. Young children, nonreaders, and English learners can draw pictures in response to oral prompts. Collect and assemble the students' words and drawings into a book they can reference whenever they are experiencing negative emotions.

	Positive Thinking	Thankfulness
What is it?	smiling being cheerful thinking of good things seeing the best in family and friends	recognizing your privileges appreciating the good people and things in your life awareness of what others have done for you
Examples	It is a beautiful sunny day today. I have such great friends. I love my dog.	I'm glad I get to teach such great students. I appreciate my parents because they are supportive. I'm grateful for my children because they bring me joy.

My Positive Thoughts

Name _____ **Date** _____

Answer these questions on a separate sheet of paper:

- What has brought me joy?

- How have I brought joy to others?

- What has brought me peace?

- How have I brought peace to others?

- What has made me laugh?

- How have I made others laugh?

- What has made me smile?

- How have I made others smile?

- What has made me stronger?

- How have I made others stronger?

- How do others help me?

- How have I helped others?

- How have others been nice to me?

- How have I been nice to others?

- When have I been brave?

- What am I hopeful about?

- What are my successes?

Help Anxious Kids in a Stressful World © David Campos and Kathleen McConnell Fad—Free Spirit Publishing

My Attitude of Gratitude

Name _____ **Date** _____

Family members I am grateful for: _____

_____

Friends I am thankful for: _____

_____

Things I am grateful for: _____

_____

My qualities that I am thankful for: _____

_____

_____

Foods I am grateful for: _____

_____

Music I am thankful for: _____

_____

Experiences I am grateful for: _____

_____

_____

Challenges I am thankful for: _____

_____

_____

Help Anxious Kids in a Stressful World © David Campos and Kathleen McConnell Fad—Free Spirit Publishing

Go, Move, Focus

DOMAINS ADDRESSED	INSTRUCTION	CBT COMPONENTS
physiological	whole group	self-monitoring, mindfulness
social and emotional	small group	

Ready

Each student's experience of anxiety is unique, so teachers and school mental health professionals need a variety of strategies to help students cope with their challenges in emotionally healthy and productive ways. This strategy combines three established techniques for managing stress responses to anxiety:

- Go: spend time outdoors
- Move: exercise
- Focus: practice mindfulness

Getting outdoors is beneficial for health and wellness. Spending time in nature can lower blood pressure, reduce the amount of stress hormones, and improve mood. Exercise has significant positive effects too. It can decrease muscle tension, which reduces the body's contribution to anxiety; can reduce the impact of persistent negative thinking on the body through the release of endorphins that serve as natural painkillers; can improve sleep; and may decrease depression. Mindfulness is a conscious awareness of the present moment and environment. Being mindful can help students accept their thoughts, feelings, and bodily sensations, which contributes to a greater sense of well-being.

Set

In this strategy, students will take a walk outdoors—on the school campus or in a nearby neighborhood—and focus on details in their environment for a few minutes. This purposeful attention will help them become more aware of their environment and less focused on their repetitive worries and fears. Make copies of the activity sheets on pages 99–101 and 102–105 (Look, Listen, Feel, and Think Cards for younger students, nonreaders, or English learners and Focus Cards for older students), and prepare to pass some out to the students. Choose the cards that match your students' needs, ages, and interests. If your students are nonreaders, you can read the cards aloud to them. On the blank cards, consider creating your own focus instructions that correspond to the community where your group will be walking. Get your school leadership team's permission to take your class for a walk around the school campus and/or nearby neighborhood. Decide where you will walk, and then set your expectations for the students. Make sure they are age and group appropriate. You might say, for example, "Stay with or within sight of the group. Focus on finding what is on your card. Then stay focused on that object for a few minutes. Breathe deeply. Limit your talk. And listen for my signal to return to inside."

Go

1. Tell the students that the purpose of the walk is to spend time with nature. Explain that focusing on the scenery and paying attention to something other than their worries can ease anxiety and relieve stress. You might say, for example, "When you're feeling anxious, you might get into a cycle of worry, and you may keep thinking about the same things over and over. This is called obsessing, and it can quickly become unpleasant. By focusing on details while walking outdoors, you can move away from unhelpful worries and thoughts that make you anxious."

2. Pass out one or more Look, Listen, Feel, and Think Cards or Focus Cards to each student.

3. Explain the activity using this script: "We are going to go outside for a ten-to-fifteen-minute walk. You cannot bring or use electronic devices on the walk. Read your card(s) beforehand, and think about what you will be looking for. Carry the card with you as you walk. Once you find what's on the card, give it your full attention. If you find yourself thinking about something else, especially something that worries or bothers you, stop walking and look at the card again. Look at your surroundings, such as the sky, the trees or plants, the ground or anything else in the environment. Then find the object on your card and concentrate intently on it. Breathe deeply. Then continue walking and, if you have another card, look for what is on it."

Look, Listen, Feel, and Think Cards

Find a cloud in the sky. What is it shaped like? Watch it for a few minutes. What shape did it change into?

Think about how the air outdoors feels different from the air indoors. Is it cooler or warmer? Have your emotions or actions changed because it's cooler or warmer? If so, how?

Find a plant. Look at its shape, color, and size. What do you like most about it? What would you name it?

Find something that looks like it doesn't belong where it is. Think about how it might have gotten there. Keep looking at it until you get a good idea. Make up a story about how it got there.

Focus on the wind. Is it blowing? How does it feel on your skin and in your hair or clothes? What does it remind you of?

How does walking make your body feel? Think about what you can see, how you are breathing, what the air feels like on your skin, and what is happening to each part of your body.

Look, Listen, Feel, and Think Cards *(Continued)*

Stand in one spot and slowly spin your body all the way until you are at your starting point. Does the sky look different depending on which way you were facing? Does the air feel different? What did you notice?

Sing, hum, or whistle a song as you walk. Even if you don't know the words, try making music. Sing, hum, or whistle to the rhythm of your walking.

Listen and look for a bird. If you see or hear one, focus on it for a minute. What color is it? How does it sound? How does the sound make you feel?

Find several surfaces close by and walk on each. For example, walk on grass, gravel, playground sand, and dirt. How different do they sound, smell, and feel?

How many trees do you see? How are they similar and different? How do they make you feel?

Look back at your school. What do you notice when you are far away from it? What do you notice when you are closer to it?

Help Anxious Kids in a Stressful World © David Campos and Kathleen McConnell Fad—Free Spirit Publishing

CONTINUED ➡

Look, Listen, Feel, and Think Cards (Continued)

What animal do you see? Watch it for a minute. Then close your eyes and picture it. Try to remember details about it.

Try skipping, hopping on one foot, or walking backward. Concentrate on one of these activities, then switch off between two of them. (For example, walk forward three steps, then hop on one foot, then repeat.)

Find as many colors as you can on your walk.

What signs of water do you see? What does the water look, sound, or smell like? How does it make you feel?

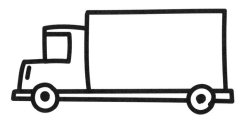

What traffic sounds do you hear? Listen for sirens, cars, horns, trucks, screeching brakes, tires crunching on rocks, and so on. Focus on one sound and see how long it lasts.

Focus Cards

Look for a cloud in the sky that reminds of you a person, place, or thing. What does it look like to you? Watch it for a few minutes. What did it change into?

How is the air outdoors different from the air inside your school or home? How is it similar? Breathe it in deeply. Is it moist or dry? Fresh or stale? Focus only on the air and describe it in your head.

Find a plant that you have never seen before. Look at the shape, the color, and the size. What are its most striking features? What would you name it?

Think about how the air temperature outdoors in this moment is different from the air temperature when you were indoors. Is it cooler or warmer? How have your emotions and actions changed because of the temperature change?

Focus on the wind for a moment. Is it blowing today? Do you feel a breeze on your face or in your hair or clothing? How does it make you feel? Can you find a tree or other plant whose leaves are blowing in the wind? Watch that plant for at least two minutes. What do you notice about it? What does it remind you of?

Find something that looks like it doesn't belong where it is. It could be a flower growing all by itself or a soft patch of grass in the middle of some weeds. Think about how it might have gotten there. Keep looking at it until you get a good idea. Focus on it and make up a story about how it got there.

Stand in one spot and slowly spin your body all the way until you are at your starting point. Do your feelings change as you look around? How?

How does walking make your body feel different from when you are sitting? What changes do you notice? Think about what you can see, how you are breathing, what the air feels like on your skin, and what is happening to each part of your body.

Focus Cards (Continued)

Stand still for a minute. Listen and look for a bird. If you see or hear one, focus on it for at least two or three minutes. What color is it? How does it sound? How does the sound make you feel?

Sing, hum, or whistle a song as you walk. Even if you don't know the words, try making music. Sing, hum, or whistle to the rhythm of your walking.

If there are trees where you are walking, how many different kinds do you see? Even if you don't know their names, identify how they are different or similar. How do they make you feel?

As you walk, try a specific breathing routine. Pick one ahead of time and practice before you start the walk. For example, breathe in for a count of seven and out for seven or breathe in for a count of four, hold for four, and breathe out for four.

Do you see any animals on this walk? Is anyone walking a dog? Do you see any squirrels? What about bugs? Find at least one animal and watch it for a minute or two. Then close your eyes and picture it. Try to remember details about it.

Before you start your walk, look for several surfaces close by and walk on each. For example, walk on grass, gravel, playground sand, and dirt. As you walk, concentrate on how different they sound, smell, and feel. How does each impact your emotions?

Focus on your breathing as you walk. Try to breathe in through your nose and out through your mouth. When you breathe in, try to expand your diaphragm (your belly) instead of your chest. Keep breathing regularly while you walk.

As you walk, focus on a rhythm. Set a comfortable pace and stick with it or walk next to someone and match your steps with theirs. How does it feel to walk in rhythm with someone else?

CONTINUED ➡

Focus Cards *(Continued)*

Try skipping, hopping on one foot, or walking backward. Concentrate on one of these, then switch off between two of them. (For example, walk forward three steps, then hop on one foot, then repeat.)

As you walk, find three things that you never thought much about before. Maybe you see a new tree or a new building. Maybe you see a path you never followed. Be on the lookout for something that has been there all along but is new to you.

Find as many colors on your walk as you can. Consider that the green of the grass is not the same shade as the green of a tennis ball.

As you walk, stop occasionally and turn in a full circle, so you can see everything all around you. Think about how much you can see from one place.

What signs of water do you see? Are there puddles, a fountain, a stream, a pond, or anything else with water? If so, what does it look, smell, or sound like? Take a few minutes to look closely at it. How does that water make you feel?

As you walk away from your school, look back at the building. How does your perspective change when you are far away instead of close? When you are walking back, do the same thing: think about how things are different when you are close versus far away. What do you notice?

What traffic sounds do you hear? Listen for sirens, horns, cars, trucks, screeching brakes, tires crunching on rocks, and so on. Focus on one sound and see how long it lasts.

As you walk leisurely outdoors, compare it to when you walk outdoors with a goal in mind, such as walking to school in the morning, walking to catch the bus, or walking to the cafeteria. What is different? How do you feel? Are you more relaxed? How does walking affect your anxiety?

CONTINUED ➡

Focus Cards *(Continued)*

Are you walking uphill, downhill, on flat ground, or a combination? How do you feel when you are walking uphill or downhill? How does your breathing change?

Try to smile at least ten times while you walk. Hum a tune or sing your favorite song; think about someone who brings you joy; think about your best day. Say to yourself repeatedly, "I feel good."

Positive Pictures for Positive Feelings

DOMAINS ADDRESSED	INSTRUCTION	CBT COMPONENTS
physiological	whole group	self-monitoring, relaxation, cognitive restructuring, visualization
social and emotional	small group	
	individual	

Ready

Affirmations and positive comments can reduce negative feelings, doubts, and worries. Likewise, visuals that portray happiness can cultivate joy and decrease anxiety. When students use uplifting pictures and photographs to reimagine their immediate surroundings, they can mentally transport themselves to a serene location. Paying close attention to such pictures may help students reframe their situation, which can trigger positive emotions.

Set

Students will be selecting age- and interest-appropriate pictures or photos for this strategy. For older students, follow the school district guidelines related to internet searches. As the students begin to select their images, double-check that their selections are acceptable and appropriate. They can look for images that evoke calm, such as empty beaches, mountains, clouds, waves, trees, flowers, birds in flight, sunrises, sunsets, or other natural scenes. For younger students, present a group of images and ask the students to select those that will help them feel positive, peaceful, or calm. Keep in mind that some students, especially those who live in urban settings, may not be familiar with nature scenes. For those students, guide them toward images of puppies or pets, children hugging their family members, stained-glass windows in a place of worship, a child in a blanket fort or curled up with a book and a flash-light. The students can use search terms such as peaceful places, calm destinations, relaxing images, or rest and calm places for the images. Closely supervise the activity as students search the following options:

■ Google images: photos specifically chosen for stress and anxiety reduction

■ free images from district-approved websites

- students' own favorite digital photos, which for older students could be on their smartphones

- simple drawings or icons that have special meaning for individual students

Then, review action strategies 1 and 2, which help students identify when they feel anxious. When students can recognize the signs of their own anxiety, they won't need adults to cue them to use this strategy.

Go

1. Allow students time to select up to ten visuals that they find calming, relaxing, and positive.

2. Have the students print or download their selected images.

3. Ask them to hole-punch the printed images on a corner and assemble them with a key ring; consolidate all the images in a personal folder; or load them into an interactive notebook or folder on a smartphone or tablet. The goal is for students to be able to access their images easily.

4. Teach the students breathing exercises to do as they view their images if they want to try this. Action Strategy 4 offers four examples.

5. When students are feeling stressed or worried, let them look at their images for a minute or two and enjoy what they see. Repeat the strategy as needed. Encourage students to use their pictures on their own, outside of school, with their families, and in other settings whenever and wherever they need to boost their positive feelings.

ACTION STRATEGY 10

Everyone Move!

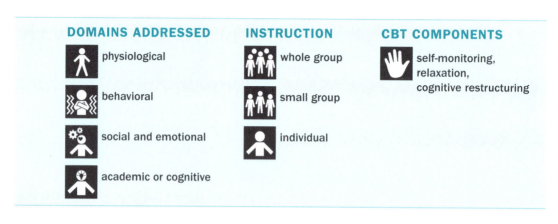

DOMAINS ADDRESSED	INSTRUCTION	CBT COMPONENTS
physiological	whole group	self-monitoring, relaxation, cognitive restructuring
behavioral	small group	
social and emotional	individual	
academic or cognitive		

Ready

Exercise has many significant health benefits. Among other things, it can decrease tension, improve mood, and relieve anxiety and depression. The changes in brain chemistry from exercising help regulate stress responses and emotional reactions and enhance executive functioning. Because people with anxiety tend to be more sedentary, interventions at school may be needed to encourage children to exercise. When the school community prioritizes movement and physical activity—in physical education, during recess, in classrooms, and in after-school programs—students get healthy in body *and* mind.

Set

Before beginning this action strategy, rearrange desks, furniture, and equipment that may prevent students from moving around the classroom safely. Also, set up your class schedule to include the exercise breaks in this strategy. Then follow these guidelines:

1. Start with exercise that is fun and easy. Remember, the exercise does not have to be rigorous or lengthy to make a difference.

2. Safety is important, so have clear rules about where and how students move. (For example: Listen and follow teacher directions, move safely in your personal space, ask questions for clarification, be brave and try the activities.) Teach and practice the rules with brief activities.

3. After you've tried the exercises in this strategy, poll the students to find out which exercises they like most. Repeat those regularly.

Later, if you find yourself looking for more movement ideas, try these resources:

- Active Schools: activeschoolsus.org/wp-content/uploads/2021/02/AC-Resources-One-Pager-for-News-and-Resources.pdf
- Playworks Game Library: playworks.org/game-library
- American Heart Association: www2.heart.org/site/DocServer/KHC_25_Ways_to_Get_Moving_at_home.pdf
- Nemours Kids Health: kidshealth.org/en/parents/elementary-exercises.html

Go

1. **Scavenger Hunt:**

   a. Give individual students or pairs of students a list of five to ten items that are in the classroom. For example, you might list a specific book, an orange item, an object made of metal, a spherical item, a writing tool, and a transparent object. If age-appropriate, consider using riddles for the listed objects. For example, you might write, "You twist and turn me to enter another dimension" to suggest a doorknob.

   b. Review the rules of the game. You might tell your students, "No grabbing from another student or taking from their desk or backpack without permission; handle the objects safely; and no going in the teacher's desk."

   c. Use a timer to limit the hunt to five to seven minutes.

   d. When the timer goes off, invite the students to explain what they found.

2. **Five Minutes, Five Movements:**

   a. Explain to your students that they will be listening to music for five minutes. Create a playlist with five different music segments, each one minute long.

   b. Start the music. Do one of the following movements for one minute, then start a different movement when the music changes:

      - Arm circles: Stretch your arms out to your sides and circle them forward, then backward. Repeat.

      - High knees: Raise your right knee, then your left knee. If you like, add an opposing elbow touch. Repeat.

      - Box move: Step forward with your right foot, then step forward with your left foot; step back with your right foot, then step back with your left foot. Repeat. Add claps up high when stepping forward, and claps down low when stepping backward.

      - Reach to the sky: Stand up and raise both hands high as though reaching to the sky. Then, stand on your tiptoes to stretch the movement. Repeat.

- Robot hops: Hop forward on two feet, then hop back. Add arm movements like this during each hop: one arm moves forward while the other moves backward. Repeat.

- Shoulder stretches: Extend your right arm to the left across your chest. Grab it with your left hand and tug it close to your body. Hold. Do the same with the left arm and right hand. Repeat. Add shoulder shrugs and rolls later.

- More stretches: Hold your arms up high. Then reach down to your knees, then your toes. Hold, then straighten and shake out your arms. Repeat.

3. **Full-Body Rock, Paper, Scissors:**

   a. Challenge your students to design three full-body movements that can represent rock, paper, and scissors. For example, *rock* might be a squat. *Paper* might be standing straight with both arms above the head. *Scissors* might be jumping in place while scissoring the arms. Part of the fun of this activity is helping students design their own movements.

   b. Have the students face off. Students line up facing each other in pairs and on the count of three, they do a rock, paper, or scissors body movement—their choice. The winning students continue challenging each other in pairs until one student is left standing.

4. Repeat these exercises whenever the students seem stressed or worried.

School Thanks

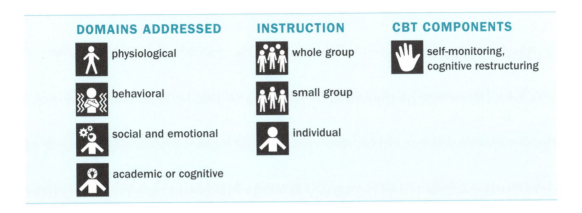

DOMAINS ADDRESSED
- physiological
- behavioral
- social and emotional
- academic or cognitive

INSTRUCTION
- whole group
- small group
- individual

CBT COMPONENTS
- self-monitoring, cognitive restructuring

Ready

When students build positive relationships with peers and teachers, they have a stronger sense of belonging, are more open to learning, are less lonely, and have higher academic achievement. In this strategy, you can encourage students to be thankful for a person, thing, or experience that happened at school. Thankfulness can help students who are worried and stressed avoid spiraling into negativity, isolation, and fear.

Set

This action strategy encourages students to express thanks for something or someone at school. Take a moment to review Action Strategy 7, which explains the difference between positive thinking (seeing the best in life) and thankfulness (appreciating good things). Then prepare enough copies of the School Thank-You Cards (pages 113–114) so you'll have at least one card for each student. Cut the cards apart. Review the sentence stems in the "Go" section to help students focus on feeling thankful.

Go

1. Discuss what it means to think positive and what it means to be thankful. See Action Strategy 7 for help distinguishing the two. Explain to your students that in this activity, they should focus on gratitude for people, things, or experiences at school. Share examples from your own school life, such as "I am thankful that the class library stays organized. I am thankful that we get to go outside for recess. I am thankful that I get to direct the choir, because I love to sing."

2. Invite students to use the following sentence stems to think about and share what people, things, or experiences at school they are grateful for. Write or display these sentence stems where the students can see them while you talk about them.

- I am grateful that _____ helped me with _____.

- I am thankful that in _____ class, _____.

- I appreciate _____ for _____.

- I am thankful that even though _____ happened, _____.

- I thank _____, who said something positive to me today.

- I am grateful that I got to _____ in _____.

- I'm thankful that I was able to _____.

- I appreciate _____ for helping me with _____ this week.

- Even though I _____, I still appreciate _____.

- I am happy that _____ did NOT happen today.

- School is a good place because _____.

3. Allow each student to select a card from the School Thank-You Cards.

4. Encourage the students to write or draw on their cards about the people, things, or experiences at school they are thankful for. Students can give their cards to the individuals they mention, or you can collect the cards and post them in the classroom to showcase the students' gratitude.

School Thank-You Cards

CONTINUED ➡

The Calm-Down Menu

DOMAINS ADDRESSED	INSTRUCTION	CBT COMPONENTS
physiological	whole group	modeling, self-monitoring, relaxation, visualization, mindfulness
behavioral	small group	
social and emotional	individual	
academic or cognitive		

Ready

Some students become so anxious at school that their anxiety hinders their academic work, social and emotional regulation, and physical well-being. When teachers and students work together, students with anxiety can learn to calm down at school. Teachers can help students recognize the signs of their anxiety, such as feeling irritable, restless, aggressive, fatigued, or tense. Educators can then guide students to develop a habit of choosing anxiety-reducing actions from a menu to help them calm down on their own or when prompted.

Set

Make sure all your students know the signs of anxiety. Any of these symptoms may be anxiety-related:

- irritability
- difficulty concentrating
- physical agitation or restlessness
- anger or aggression
- fatigue
- muscle tension
- excessive worrying
- preoccupation with one thing, idea, or topic
- perfectionism
- avoidance of people or situations
- refusal to engage in assignments

Before students can use the Calm-Down Menu successfully, you must prepare them:

1. Teach them to either ask for an opportunity to calm down or follow your instructions when you direct them to use the Calm-Down Menu.

2. Model each of the options on the Calm-Down Menu.

3. Give students a chance to practice calming down.

Go

1. Set aside a quiet space in your classroom for the students to use as a calm-down area. Post the Calm-Down Menu and supply the area with the items mentioned in the menu. Do not use this area for exclusion or as a consequence for misbehavior. Its sole purpose is to help students calm down and prevent escalation.

2. Explain the Calm-Down Menu activity sheet to students. Model each option so that the students understand their choices. Invite them to demonstrate the options to you. For younger students, nonreaders, and English learners, consider providing images to represent the options. You can use these images as reminders and prompts.

3. Ask the students to tell you when they need to use the Calm-Down Menu. Give each student one of the Calm-Down Cue Cards (cut apart from the activity sheet on page 118), which they can use to signal their need to calm down. You might also consider other options, such as placing a colored card on the desk or using a hand signal.

4. Let students visit the calm-down area whenever they need it and use the options listed on the menu. If they need help remembering what to do, take the time to provide it. After five minutes, check in with students to make sure they are calm and ready to focus before asking them to return to their seats.

Calm-Down Menu

Name _____   **Date** _____

Set the timer for five minutes. Choose how you want to calm down.

- Do a deep breathing exercise, such as Belly Breathing, 4-4-4 Breathing, Kiss Breathing, or Blow-Out-the-Candles Breathing.

- Put on headphones and listen to a calm-down playlist.

- Do some five-minute exercises, such as arm circles, stretches, lifting your knees high, or another exercise you know.

- Count backward from 100.

- Count all the small pompoms in a jar.

- Close your eyes and put your head down.

- Play with clay, slime, or a fidget toy.

- Look at pictures you've chosen to help you calm down.

- Write down all the words that name what you are feeling.

- Hold a stuffed animal.

- Look at pictures in a book.

- Squeeze and play with stress balls.

- Color, draw, write in a journal, or write a thank-you card.

Help Anxious Kids in a Stressful World © David Campos and Kathleen McConnell Fad—Free Spirit Publishing

Calm-Down Cue Cards

I need to calm down.

I need to calm down.

I need to calm down.

I need to calm down.

I need to calm down.

I need to calm down.

I need to calm down.

I need to calm down.

I need to calm down.

I need to calm down.

Coping Toolbox

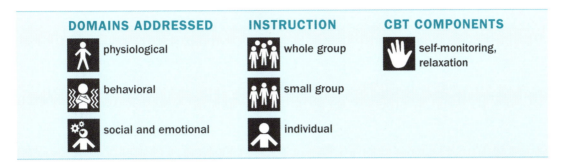

DOMAINS ADDRESSED	INSTRUCTION	CBT COMPONENTS
physiological	whole group	self-monitoring, relaxation
behavioral	small group	
social and emotional	individual	

Ready

For students with anxiety, the school day can seem long and filled with one stressful event after another. Academic and social demands (such as answering questions out loud, solving math problems on the board, or working in group activities) can trigger physiological, social, and emotional reactions in students who have anxiety. Those reactions can lead to behavioral symptoms such as restlessness, agitation, social withdrawal, and reduced ability to function at school. To help your students manage their stress, emotions, and reactions, you can provide them with a coping toolbox.

Set

A coping toolbox works much like the Calm-Down Menu in Action Strategy 12. Instead of a menu, you can use a lunchbox, shoebox, or plastic container to hold items that help students calm down and regain composure. These items should be age appropriate and require no introductions or directions. You might include strings; rubber bands; small plush or rubber toys; cubes or other hand puzzles; markers or colored pencils with a small notebook; head-phones; a short book; a list of calming affirmations; a sand timer; homemade or commercial slime, play dough, or magic sand; or Silly Putty. Take care not to overwhelm students with too many choices. You may want to rotate items in the Coping Toolbox to see what works best and to prevent boredom or overuse.

Go

1. Explain the rules for accessing the Coping Toolbox. For example: (a) Ask the teacher for a Coping Toolbox. (b) Take it to your desk. (c) Set the sand timer. (d) Use the items quietly. (e) Use one item at a time. (f) Return the box quietly when your time is up.

2. Designate a time limit for using the Coping Toolbox that is age appropriate and prevents lost instructional time. A sand timer can help the students manage their time.

3. Make the toolbox accessible to the students under the conditions you have set for them.

4. At some point after student use, follow up with the student to determine if the toolbox helped them calm down. Ask about preferred items to include in the toolbox.

5. Add or remove items as needed. Consider rotating items with things students bring from home.

A Team of Friends

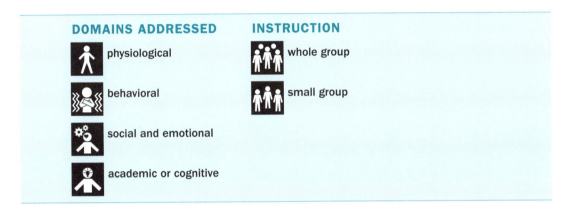

DOMAINS ADDRESSED

- physiological
- behavioral
- social and emotional
- academic or cognitive

INSTRUCTION

- whole group
- small group

Ready

When students get to know one another, they not only learn about others' personalities, backgrounds, strengths, weaknesses, and so forth, they also discover mutual interests, which are the foundation for building and keeping friendships. Most students do care about one another; they want to be accepted and supported; and they want help from and want to help others. The support and friendship students get from their peers can help them cope with bouts of worry, stress, and anxiety.

Set

This action strategy works on the premise that having a team of friends who are classmates enriches students' lives and provides support whenever they experience challenging moments. Before starting this strategy, discuss with your students the benefits of having a team of friends:

- The team can help you celebrate good times and support you during bad times.
- The team can bring you happiness.
- The team can reduce your stress.
- The team can encourage you to make decisions that help you.
- The team can help you feel that you belong.
- The team can give you advice and encouragement.

In the discussion, point out that *all* students in the class form a team of friends. For the activity, sort students into smaller teams.

Go

1. Challenge each team of students to work together to design a team shield using one copy of the Our Team Shield activity sheet on page 123. This can help them develop a stronger sense of team membership with shared values, such as:

   - helping one another

   - supporting one another

   - treating one another with kindness and understanding

   - avoiding ridicule, meanness, and verbal or nonverbal aggression

2. Explain to your students that when they feel anxious, they may need support. Give examples of anxiety-related behaviors, such as:

   - fidgeting and having trouble concentrating

   - getting very quiet and/or withdrawing from others

   - having trouble breathing

   - worrying about things that probably won't happen

   - repeating the same behaviors over and over

   - trying hard to be perfect at everything

3. Together as a class, complete the How We Help a Friend Menu (page 124) using words or pictures. The supports on the menu might include actions such as listening, reminding the classmate to relax or breathe deeply, or saying an encouraging word. A sample menu appears here. Post your menu in a visible spot in the classroom.

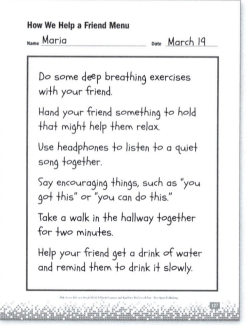

4. Give each student a copy of the I Need a Friend Cue Cards (page 125). Tell students they can cut up these cards and hand them to you whenever they feel they need a friend because they feel anxious, they feel that they are losing control, or they are getting stuck in negative thinking.

5. When a student gives you a cue card, hand it to a classmate who can help and instruct that student to take any of the actions listed on the How We Help a Friend Menu. The pair may need to move to a corner of the classroom, the hallway, or somewhere else that is quiet and safe.

6. Use a timer to remind the pair when to return.

Our Team Shield

Name _____   **Date** _____

How We Help a Friend Menu

Name _____ **Date** _____

I Need a Friend Cue Cards

I need a friend right now.

I need a friend right now.

I need a friend right now.

I need a friend right now.

I need a friend right now.

I need a friend right now.

Box of Worries

DOMAINS ADDRESSED	INSTRUCTION	CBT COMPONENTS
physiological	whole group	self-monitoring, relaxation, mindfulness
behavioral	small group	
social and emotional	individual	
academic or cognitive		

Ready

Students with anxiety often have overwhelming worries that lead to behavioral symptoms, such as restlessness, fidgeting, social withdrawal, and irritability, that prevent them from participating in group activities or completing their assignments. These symptoms may be upsetting for students and difficult for teachers to manage. This strategy can help reduce worrying in students who tend to worry about academic performance, social relationships, and what is happening in their world.

Set

Find an empty cardboard box for your Box of Worries. Label it and, if you like, decorate the box to catch your students' attention. Explain to your students that the purpose of the box is to allow them to express their worries and then store them away for a while. Make multiple copies of the My Worry Card activity sheet (page 128). Each sheet includes two cards, so cut the sheets in half. Place the cards near the Box of Worries in an accessible spot in the classroom.

Go

1. Discuss these aspects of worrying:

- Everyone worries.
- It's okay to worry about *some* things *some*times.
- You can change some of things you worry about, but not everything you worry about.

- When you worry too much about things you can't control, this can make you feel worse instead of better.

- Worrying doesn't change the outcome of a situation.

- If your worrying keeps you from getting your work done, enjoying your friends and family, or having fun, then you are probably worrying too much.

- By writing down your worries and putting them away for a while, you might be able to worry less and have a good day at school.

2. Explain that writing down worries and/or talking them over with someone can help reduce worrying.

3. Give each student a copy of My Worry Card and tell them they can write their worries on a card whenever they want and put their completed cards in the Box of Worries. They do not have to write their names on the cards unless they want to, and they can mark whether they want their worry discussed with the class. Explain that teachers are required by law to report suspected cases of abuse and neglect to the local child protection or law enforcement agency.

4. Emphasize that writing down worries won't make them go away forever, but putting them away for a while and focusing on school activities may reduce worrying and help students feel better.

5. After students put their worries in the Box of Worries, encourage them not to think about their worries for the rest of the day.

6. When the opportunity arises, review the cards in the box. Discuss these worries as a group. Ask students to suggest coping strategies. If many students have the same worries, set up a time for a counselor to visit the class. Do not disclose information that can be linked with specific students.

7. If a card says a student wants to talk to someone privately about their worries, set up a meeting with or for that student.

8. Check the Box of Worries daily.

My Worry Card

My Worry Card

I am worried about: _____

_____

It's okay to discuss my worry with the class: ☐ yes ☐ no

I would like to talk about my worry with someone: ☐ yes ☐ no

This is the teacher or school specialist I want to talk to: _____

My name is (write only if you want): _____

I'm going try hard not to think about my worry when it is in the Box of Worries.

My Worry Card

I am worried about: _____

_____

It's okay to discuss my worry with the class: ☐ yes ☐ no

I would like to talk about my worry with someone: ☐ yes ☐ no

This is the teacher or school specialist I want to talk to: _____

My name is (write only if you want): _____

I'm going try hard not to think about my worry when it is in the Box of Worries.

Gratitude Journal

DOMAINS ADDRESSED	INSTRUCTION	CBT COMPONENTS
physiological	whole group	self-monitoring, cognitive restructuring
social and emotional	small group	
	individual	

Ready

Action Strategy 7 (Thanks for Three) and Action Strategy 11 (School Thanks) can get students started on recognizing and expressing gratitude for the positives in their lives. Keeping a gratitude journal is another strategy that can help your students focus on positive thinking and thankfulness. It can improve mental well-being, reduce stress and anxiety, strengthen relationships, increase optimism and peace of mind, reduce ruminating (repeated thinking over the same thing), improve sleep, and increase energy.

Set

Set guidelines for writing in gratitude journals that fit your students' age, grade level, and maturity. For example, very young students can complete a drawing once or twice a week showing what they are grateful for. Older students can write one to three sentences daily that explain what they are thankful for and why. Gather ideas in your mind to explain why expressing gratitude is a healthy habit. For example, focusing on the good things in life often leads to positive thinking, which contributes to higher energy levels, faster healing from illness or injury, and better coping skills. Practicing gratitude has similar boosting effects that contribute to overall happiness.

Go

1. Discuss the benefits of practicing gratitude. See strategies 7 and 11 for ideas.

2. Brainstorm with students the areas of their lives they could consider for practicing gratitude. For example, create a chart on the board like the following one and invite your students to contribute what they are thankful for in each column. For younger students, focus on just one or two areas—perhaps home and school.

Personal Health	Home	School	Community	Country and World
My glasses help me see better. I'm getting braces!	I love my sister. My mom takes me to school each morning. My dad is awesome!	Mr. A's science class is the best! PE is fun. I get to eat with my friends each day.	They're extending the bike trail.	We live in the best country in the world.

3. Decide on a journal format. An internet search will show many examples of gratitude journals that you can easily replicate. Let the students decide whether they'd like to keep monthly, weekly, or daily journals. You can create gratitude journals by stapling single sheets of paper together or using composition books, daily planners, or blank diaries. Students could even share their ideas in more visual ways, such as a gratitude paper chain across the room or a bulletin board full of gratitude drawings. The activity sheets on pages 131 and 132 are two more options. Young children, nonreaders, and English learners can draw, describe orally, and work with partners. Today I Am Grateful provides prompts and lines for writing, and I Am Thankful Today provides prompts and space for drawings.

4. Determine a regular schedule for students to write in their journals. Explain to them that they can first focus on small events or acts (for example, "I'm grateful for my phone") and then work toward larger, more elaborate ideas (for example, "Dolly Parton is not just a wonderful singer; she is a great humanitarian too").

5. Review the journal entries with individual students or in groups to process their reflections. If you're discussing in groups, be sure to respect students' privacy. During the discussion, emphasize specific comments that demonstrate positive thinking, imagery, and self-talk that contribute to happiness.

Today I Am Grateful

Name _____ **Date** _____

Today, I am grateful for: _____

_____

Because: _____

_____

_____

_____

_____

_____

_____

_____

Help Anxious Kids in a Stressful World © David Campos and Kathleen McConnell Fad—Free Spirit Publishing

I Am Thankful Today

Name _____   **Date** _____

I am thankful today for: _____

Help Anxious Kids in a Stressful World © David Campos and Kathleen McConnell Fad—Free Spirit Publishing

Yet and Right Now

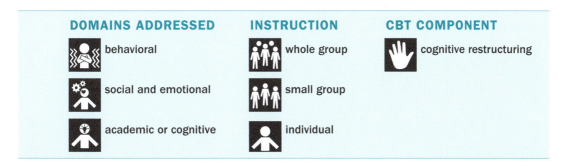

DOMAINS ADDRESSED
- behavioral
- social and emotional
- academic or cognitive

INSTRUCTION
- whole group
- small group
- individual

CBT COMPONENT
- cognitive restructuring

Ready

Students with anxiety often have unfounded and unreasoned negative thoughts about themselves. These thoughts can lead students to behave in unproductive and self-harming ways. They might withdraw in class, give up easily on assignments, worry excessively over people and events they cannot control, and experience physical ailments. These behaviors and experiences, in turn, can negatively impact students' social relationships, academic functioning, and emotional well-being, which can lead to feeling even worse about themselves and consequently more anxious.

Set

This action strategy helps students replace negative thoughts with realistic alternatives. Action Strategy 3, What Not to Think, discusses four types of thinking that can intensify anxiety: catastrophizing, all-or-nothing thinking, mind reading, and fortune-telling. Review these prior to discussing with your students the patterns and repercussions of negative thinking. Challenge students to use the words *yet* and *right now* whenever they begin to have negative thoughts.

Go

1. Encourage students to start modifying their critical comments about themselves or their situations by adding the words *yet* or *right now*.

2. Prepare a chart on a whiteboard, bulletin board, or flip chart with the headings "Instead of . . ." on the left and "Say . . ." on the right. Underneath the headings, write the following examples to get students thinking and talking about shifting their inner dialogue to be more positive.

Instead of...	Say...
I'll never finish this work. It's too hard.	I haven't finished this work YET.
No one likes me because I'm not cool.	People don't know me YET, but they'll think I'm cool when they do.
My mom might lose her job.	RIGHT NOW Mom has a job, and we're okay.
I never have any spending money.	RIGHT NOW I don't have spending money, but I will when I'm older and I get a job.
I can't memorize this formula. It's too hard.	I haven't memorized this formula YET.
I'll bet I fail this test.	I don't know this information YET, but I can learn it for the test.

3. Print several copies of the Yet! and Right Now! Cue Cards on page 135. Cut apart the cards and keep them handy in your classroom. When a student uses negative self-talk, hand them a cue card to help them practice shifting their inner dialogue. You can support younger students by using the following strategies:

◾ Assign student partners. Tell students that they can help their partners by cueing them to use their Yet! and Right Now! Cue Cards. They can keep the cards within reach at their seats. If a student hears their partner make a negative or hopeless self-statement, they can hand the partner a card and cue them to try again.

◾ During circle time or as part of a transition, ask students to share one thing that was difficult for them, but that they did anyway. Give an example to get them started and keep it simple. (For example, "I always have trouble with spelling words, but I wrote the best sentence I could *right now*.")

4. Consider inviting half the students in the class to think up a negative thought together and say it out loud. Challenge the other half of the class to work together to rephrase the negative statement using the words *yet* or *right now*.

Yet! and Right Now! Cue Cards

YET!	RIGHT NOW!
YET!	RIGHT NOW!
YET!	RIGHT NOW!
YET!	RIGHT NOW!
YET!	RIGHT NOW!

Working in Twos

DOMAINS ADDRESSED	INSTRUCTION	CBT COMPONENTS
behavioral	whole group	exposure, modeling
social and emotional	small group	
academic or cognitive		

Ready

A primary feature of social anxiety is worrying about public embarrassment, such as not knowing the answer when called on in class, appearing foolish in front of peers, or being judged harshly by others. This excessive worry can hinder academic and social functioning, which in turn can jump-start a vicious cycle of more worry, followed by impaired performance, which leads to more worry, and so forth. This action strategy includes three instructional structures designed to prevent the excessive worrying associated with social anxiety.

Set

While you should expect students to perform individually sometimes, taking the stress out of public responses in other situations can bring out the best in all students. Following are three question-and-answer structures—Even/Odd Partners, Quick Check Cards, and Scoot!—that pair students to work together and support each other rather than shining a spotlight on individuals.

Go

1. Alternate between these three question-and-answer structures when you're reviewing content for an exam or asking critical thinking questions as part of a formative assessment.

■ **Even/Odd Partners**

   a. Create a list of questions so that each student has at least one to answer.

   b. Give each student a question before beginning the lesson. Give even-numbered questions to half the class and odd-numbered questions to the other half.

c. Allow students a minute or two to think about the questions and answers.

d. Pair students who have even-numbered questions with students who have odd-numbered questions.

e. Give the pairs a few minutes to discuss their answers and offer suggestions.

f. Allow each pair to present their questions and answers out loud to the whole group, clarifying their responses as needed.

■ **Quick Check Cards**

a. Create a list of questions so that each student has at least one to answer.

b. Print a copy of the Quick Check Cards activity sheet (page 138) and cut apart the cards. Write a question on a card (or on a strip of paper).

c. Hand a card to each student.

d. After students read their cards and think about the question, ask them to note on their cards whether they want to answer the question out loud. They can write their answer on the back of the card.

e. Pair students who have even-numbered questions with students who have odd-numbered questions.

f. Give the paired students time to answer their questions.

g. Gather all the cards and call on the students who say they are comfortable answering out loud. Allow the pair to answer together if they prefer.

■ **Scoot!**

a. Count your questions and gather that many sheets of blank paper. Write one question on each sheet of paper and post the questions around the room.

b. You should have enough questions for each pair to answer a question. (For example, if you have thirty students, you need at least fifteen questions.)

c. Pair the students and give each pair a clipboard with a sheet of paper on which to write answers to all the questions. Assign all the pairs to start at different questions.

d. Give the pairs enough time to answer a question before calling out "Scoot!" When you call out, the pairs must move on to the next question in a clockwise fashion. The pairs continue progressing to the next question each time you tell them to scoot, until they have finished answering all the questions.

2. After the question-and-answer period, debrief with students to clear up misunderstandings, emphasize key points, or review information that students find challenging to learn.

Quick Check Cards

✓ **QUICK CHECK**

Question: _____

_____

_____

Do you want to answer out loud?

☐ yes ☐ no

Name: _____

Who do you want to tag for help?

_____

✓ **QUICK CHECK**

Question: _____

_____

_____

Do you want to answer out loud?

☐ yes ☐ no

Name: _____

Who do you want to tag for help?

_____

✓ **QUICK CHECK**

Question: _____

_____

_____

Do you want to answer out loud?

☐ yes ☐ no

Name: _____

Who do you want to tag for help?

_____

✓ **QUICK CHECK**

Question: _____

_____

_____

Do you want to answer out loud?

☐ yes ☐ no

Name: _____

Who do you want to tag for help?

_____

Check-Ins That Work

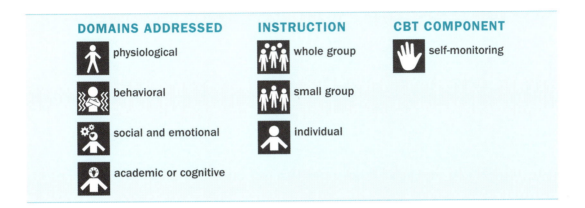

DOMAINS ADDRESSED

physiological

behavioral

social and emotional

academic or cognitive

INSTRUCTION

whole group

small group

individual

CBT COMPONENT

self-monitoring

Ready

It is nearly impossible to know how every student is doing emotionally, physically, behaviorally, and academically all the time. Because anxious students are often reluctant to initiate conversations or share about their personal lives, check-ins can be useful tools for gauging their mental health.

Set

Check-ins should be quick and easy, and they should obtain enough information from students so you can determine with reasonable accuracy how they are feeling; what concerns, fears, or worries they have; if they want to share anything with you or another caring adult; if they are experiencing a crisis of any kind; how teachers, counselors, or others can help; and if they need help immediately.

Go

1. Ask students, "How are you feeling?" Show the How Are You Feeling? chart on page 141 so students can see the variety of emotions they may be feeling and choose from them. For younger children, nonreaders, or English learners, you can read the emotion words as you point to the pictures.

2. Use the My Check-In form on page 142 to help students understand the emotions they're feeling and how they might address these emotions. You can read the prompts aloud to young students, nonreaders, and English learners.

3. Encourage students to use the How Are You Feeling? chart and the My Check-In form daily.

4. Review your students' responses and follow up with students who are not doing well, who want to talk, or who have a problem. If you notice patterns of excessive stress, worry, and anxiety, share anxiety-reducing action strategies.

How Are You Feeling?

Name _____   **Date** _____

happy

disappointed

elated

angry

hopeful

exhausted

mischievous

meh

dismayed

scared

upset

silly

overwhelmed

anxious

content

relieved

delighted

excited

surprised

ill

guilty

sad

loved

bored

sleepy

My Check-In

Name _____ **Date** _____

I am feeling _____

I have felt this way before: ☐ yes ☐ no

I need help with a coping strategy: ☐ yes ☐ no

I need to talk to you: ☐ yes ☐ no

I have been using these strategies to help myself:

    ☐ breathing exercises

    ☐ positive self-talk

    ☐ listening to calming music

    ☐ spending quiet time looking at photos that I like

    ☐ writing in my journal

    ☐ talking with a friend

    ☐ asking my friends for help

    ☐ asking a trusted adult for help

    ☐ other: _____

Visual Cue Cards

DOMAINS ADDRESSED	INSTRUCTION	CBT COMPONENTS
behavioral	individual	 self-monitoring, cognitive restructuring
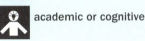 academic or cognitive		

Ready

When students are anxious, they often have difficulty focusing on assignments, concentrating on lessons, remembering important information, and staying organized. Visual supports (images on cards that are used as cues, prompts, and reminders) can be helpful for students experiencing anxiety. Visual supports are simple to use, can prevent more intensive interventions, and allow you to attend easily to specific students who need support to stay on task.

Set

Use visual supports for individual students who consistently have difficulty with attention, self-control, organization, and other executive functioning skills. Use images to assist them with specific behaviors and/or skills, such as asking for help, focusing on assignments, listening, staying positive, and not giving up. Print copies of the Visual Cue Cards activity sheet (pages 144–145) and cut the cards apart.

Go

1. Identify the students whose anxiety leads them to behave in unproductive ways. These are often students who get easily frustrated, shut down, and stop working.

2. Select a Visual Cue Card that matches an anxious student's behavior. For example, if the student gives up easily, then select a card that conveys "keep trying." If none of the provided cards match a student's behavior, draw your own simple, clear, and if possible humorous image on one of the blank cards. Add a word or simple phrase if you like.

3. Explain to the student that you will use this cue card as a quiet reminder to work on the needed skill.

4. Place the cue card in front of the student whenever they need a reminder.

5. Address just one or two behaviors at a time. More than that may overwhelm the student.

Visual Cue Cards

Ask for help.

Keep going!

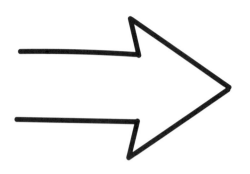

Take a deep breath.

Slow down.

Think positive.

Listen to others.

CONTINUED ➡

Visual Cue Cards *(Continued)*

Keep trying!

You've got this!

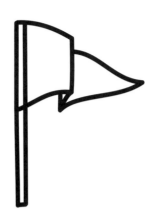

Stop a minute, then
start again.

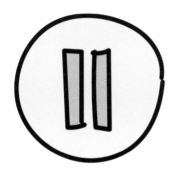

Focus.

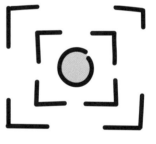

Visual Scheduling

DOMAINS ADDRESSED

 behavioral

 academic or cognitive

INSTRUCTION

 whole group

 small group

CBT COMPONENT

 self-monitoring

Ready

Action Strategy 20 (Visual Cue Cards) provides instructional support for individual students who need help with academic and/or behavioral skills when their anxiety starts to interfere with their functioning. This action strategy describes a way to offer group visual support focused on scheduling.

Anxiety appears or grows in students when they judge a situation, event, or person as unpredictable or unfamiliar. Knowing in advance what to expect in the classroom can be reassuring. Schedules and routines are critical tools for anxious students.

Set

Visible, easy to understand, and efficient schedules provide structure in the classroom and lead to routines that ward off uncertainty and help students make concrete decisions. For example, when students know that snack time occurs daily at 10:00 a.m., they are more likely to bring food from home and count on eating it at that specific time. Moreover, visual schedules can help students manage their time to complete tasks as needed. The visual schedule for your class should match your students' ages, independence levels, and maturity. The premise of a visual schedule is to make a class period or school day simpler and less stressful.

Go

1. Determine how you will present your schedule visually. Simple signage that all students can see from their seats works best.

2. Decide how much information to include in your schedule. If you're an elementary teacher or have a self-contained classroom, organize the day's schedule by content area. Include breaks, lunch, and other social periods. If you're a middle school teacher or

teach in a content-based classroom, sequence the class period activities for the whole class and for small groups. For example:

- 9:00—Take out interactive notebooks and answer the challenging questions.
- 9:05—direct instruction
- 9:25—group work
- 9:40—independent work time
- 9:55—closing statements and content connections
- 9:59—Skedaddle.

Consider adding more information to pique students' interest (for example, spotlight on a student or famous person), to develop students' skills (such as a metacognitive question for the day: "Can you provide me more information?"), or to address an instructional standard (for example, daily sentence diagramming).

3. Put as much information on the visual schedule as students need to feel comfortable knowing what will happen, but not so much information that they are overwhelmed. Consider including:

- a summary of the topics, assignments, and expected outcomes
- transitions from one topic, assignment, or subject area to the next
- notifications of changes
- behavior expectations and guidelines
- upcoming assignments and activities
- messages about teamwork, motivation, or cooperation

4. If you're a middle grade teacher, you might also create and post a large monthly schedule that emphasizes instructional standards, topics of discussion, homework, and tests or quizzes.

5. As an option for older students, provide copies of the Our Daily Schedule activity sheet (for self-contained classrooms) or the Our Weekly Schedule activity sheet (for content classes) so that they can create their own schedules to keep in their assignment notebooks.

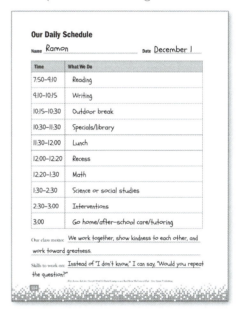

Our Daily Schedule

Name _____   Date _____

Time	What We Do

Our class motto: _____

_____

Skills to work on: _____

_____

Help Anxious Kids in a Stressful World © David Campos and Kathleen McConnell Fad—Free Spirit Publishing

Our Weekly Schedule

Name _____ **Date** _____

Day of the Week	Topic	Homework
Monday Date:		
Tuesday Date:		
Wednesday Date:		
Thursday Date:		
Friday Date:		

Help Anxious Kids in a Stressful World © David Campos and Kathleen McConnell Fad—Free Spirit Publishing

De-Stress Your Directions

DOMAINS ADDRESSED	INSTRUCTION	CBT COMPONENTS
physiological	whole group	exposure, modeling
behavioral	small group	
social and emotional		
academic or cognitive		

Ready

The school day presents many potential stressors for anxious students. Lessons can trigger anxiety in students when they have difficulty understanding and remembering information presented quickly and orally; working closely with others they do not know well; doing an assignment in an unfamiliar format; knowing what the outcome should look like; and finishing their work within an expected period. These difficulties can lead to stress reactions, such as shallow breathing, flushed skin, refusal to make eye contact or talk, racing thoughts and speech, and refusing to participate in activities. In short, the simple act of a teacher giving an assignment may result in physiological, behavioral, social and emotional, and academic or cognitive reactions for anxious students. If you work with young students, nonreaders, or English learners, consider the following additional supports. They're not only good instructional practices, they can also build students' confidence and reduce their anxiety:

- **Slow down.** Many teachers talk too fast.
- **Wait.** Many teachers expect action too quickly after giving a direction. Wait. Let it sink in.
- **Use visual cues.** Cues can be simple, such as students holding up a forefinger to signify a quick review of directions or holding up two fingers for an example of the teacher's expectation. Cues can also be more involved, as when teachers present a sample of a completed assignment so that students get a visual idea of what their final product might look like.

- **Consider partners.** Not every assignment can be a group or partner activity, but for young students and nonreaders, partners can boost confidence. Rotate partner assignments regularly.

Then, try the specific strategies that follow.

Set

The good news is that *how* you give directions can minimize stress for your students who have anxiety or other issues that affect listening, memory, direction-following, and working with others. As you read the following strategies to de-stress your directions, consider whether you want to use one consistently, combine two or more, or modify one to fit your teaching style.

Go

1. Read the following strategies for de-stressing your directions and select one to use.

- **Use a Signal**
  a. Before giving a direction, signal students to look at you and listen. The signal can be a sound (a bell or gong), a phrase *(One, two, three—look at me.)*, a hand motion (an open palm held high), or anything that works for you and your students.

  b. Use the signal consistently.

  c. Wait for all students' attention before beginning.

- **Tell Them**
  a. Tell your students what you're about to tell them. (For example: "In a moment, I'm going to tell you that I expect at least five sentences in your paragraphs.")

  b. Then tell them your message. ("You need at least five sentences in your paragraphs.")

  c. Then tell your students what you just told them. ("I just told you that I expect you to have at least five sentences in your paragraphs.")

- **Chunk It**
  a. Break the assignment into chunks.

  b. Present the first directions for the first chunk and show a completed example.

  c. Check in as your students complete the first chunk.

  d. Present the second directions for the second chunk and show a completed example.

  e. Check in as your students complete the second chunk.

  f. Continue with this process until your students have finished the assignment.

■ **Students Retell**

a. Give your students directions in three steps. As you describe the steps, hold up one finger, then two, then three.

b. Ask one student to tell you the first step. (For example: "Hector, what's the first thing you are going to do?") Do the same for the second and third steps.

c. Recite the steps again, holding up one finger, then two, then three, asking students to repeat each one after you say it.

■ **Silly Voices**

a. Select a student ahead of time and tell them the directions before you begin.

b. Explain the directions in three steps.

c. Ask the selected student to say the directions with a silly voice, such as a robot voice or a squeaky mouse voice.

d. If you'd like, call on other students to say the directions in different silly voices.

■ **Echo**

a. Select the three students before you explain the directions.

b. Explain the directions in three steps.

c. Ask the selected students to echo you after you say each step.

2. Tell your students that you plan to be more thoughtful about how you give directions, and name the strategy you will use.

3. Explain the strategy.

4. After using the strategy several times, ask the students to tell you how well it worked for them.

5. Select another strategy and repeat the process as often as you like.

Previews

DOMAINS ADDRESSED	INSTRUCTION	CBT COMPONENTS
behavioral	whole group	exposure, modeling
academic or cognitive	small group	
	individual	

Ready

For anxious students, anticipating a challenging situation is often worse than the actual occurrence. One way to reduce anxiety associated with such anticipation is to preview what's coming so that students know what to expect and can ask for help ahead of time. Teachers can offer students previews of tests, assignments, activities, schedule changes, special events, school personnel changes, and any other situations that can cause worry or stress.

Set

Predictable routines, directions, and schedules in the classroom can significantly reduce anxiety in children. Previews contribute to predictability, giving students a glimpse of what is going to happen and time to familiarize themselves with an idea and mentally prepare for it. (See also Action Strategy 21, which suggests scheduling ideas that can help students see what is coming in a week or month.)

Go

1. Read the following preview options and select one to use.

   ■ **Give a Pretest**

   a. Give students a pretest as a homework assignment before the actual test or quiz.

   b. Include page or paragraph numbers or chapter or section titles of important information, a list of key words to study, and priority labels.

   c. If you like, have students pair up and grade each other's work.

- **Coming Soon!**

   a. Briefly explain upcoming lessons, assignments, projects, tests, and events.

   b. Provide copies of the Coming Soon! activity sheet on page 155 to students so they can write or draw about the upcoming items and keep these notes in an interactive or paper assignment notebook.

- **Videos, Images, and Music**

   a. Before you teach a lesson, play music or show videos or images related to the content you will be teaching in that lesson.

   b. Show or play the media a second or third time, if you like.

   c. Give students copies of the Mystery Lesson activity sheet on page 156. Challenge them to use this form to deduce the content of the next lesson. Students can write or draw their answers.

   d. After students have made their best guesses, explain how the media relates to the upcoming lesson.

- **Today, You're Going to . . .**

   a. At the beginning of the period or day, display the activity sheet Today, You're Going to . . . (page 157) using a projector.

   b. Check off the applicable items on the list while you explain what the students will do that period or day.

- **Tomorrow, I'm Going to . . .**

   a. Near the end of the period or day, display the activity sheet Tomorrow, I'm Going to . . . (page 158) using a projector.

   b. Check off the applicable items on the list while you explain your plans for the next day.

   c. Start the next day by reviewing the items that you checked off the day before and explaining what you plan to do on this day.

2. Tell the students that you plan to preview lessons, assignments, and tests regularly and will use a specific approach.

3. Name and explain the approach.

4. After using the approach several times, ask the students to evaluate how well it worked for them.

5. Select another approach if you like.

6. Keep in mind that young children may need reminders about changes. Whenever possible, provide visuals for young children, nonreaders, and English learners.

Coming Soon!

Name _____   **Date** _____

	Lessons
	Assignments
	Projects
	Tests
	Events

Mystery Lesson

Name _____ **Date** _____

The standard we are learning:

The clue(s) our teacher showed or played for us:

The next lesson is about:

Help Anxious Kids in a Stressful World © David Campos and Kathleen McConnell Fad—Free Spirit Publishing

Today, You're Going to . . .

- ❏ answer questions
- ❏ solve problems
- ❏ answer questions out loud
- ❏ read out loud
- ❏ work by yourself
- ❏ work in groups
- ❏ work in pairs
- ❏ have
  - ❏ light homework
  - ❏ medium homework
  - ❏ heavy homework
- ❏ have a
  - ❏ test
  - ❏ quiz
- ❏ speak in front of the class
- ❏ watch a video
- ❏ listen to music
- ❏ look at some images
- ❏ be creative

- ❏ start a project
- ❏ go to the library
- ❏ go outside
- ❏ listen to a guest speaker
- ❏ have some free time
- ❏ have a snack in class
- ❏ have a drink in class
- ❏ other: _____
  _____
- ❏ other: _____
  _____
- ❏ other: _____
  _____

Tomorrow, I'm Going to . . .

❏ give you _____

❏ ask you to read out loud

❏ ask you questions to answer out loud

❏ have you work by yourself

❏ ask that you bring a library book or personal book to class

❏ put you into groups to work

❏ put you into pairs to work

❏ give you a
   ❏ light homework assignment
   ❏ medium homework assignment
   ❏ heavy homework assignment

❏ give you a
   ❏ test
   ❏ quiz

❏ ask you to speak in front of the class

❏ play a video

❏ play music

❏ show you some images

❏ give you time to be creative

❏ assign you a project

❏ take you to the library

❏ take you outside

❏ have a guest speaker

❏ give you some free time

❏ let you snack in class

❏ let you have a drink in class

❏ other: _____

_____

❏ other: _____

_____

❏ other: _____

_____

❏ other: _____

_____

❏ other: _____

_____

Help Anxious Kids in a Stressful World © David Campos and Kathleen McConnell Fad—Free Spirit Publishing

Step-by-Step Project Planners

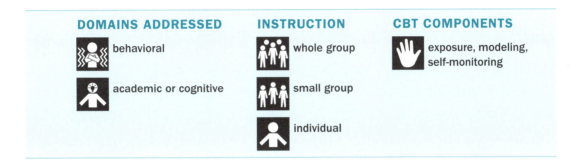

DOMAINS ADDRESSED
- behavioral
- academic or cognitive

INSTRUCTION
- whole group
- small group
- individual

CBT COMPONENTS
- exposure, modeling, self-monitoring

Ready

One of the key features of anxiety is worry. Anxious students often worry excessively about many things, especially matters they have little control over. Their anxiety can lead to frustration, procrastination, withdrawal, giving up, failing to complete tasks, and disengagement from you and their peers. This action strategy is focused on helping anxious students plan and manage long-term or multifaceted assignments, such as book reports, science construction models and experiments, research-based papers and presentations, and fine arts projects.

Set

This action strategy includes five planning tools designed to help students break down projects into manageable parts and organize their work. Choose the planning tool that best fits the project you've assigned to your students.

Go

1. After you have developed the project requirements, choose an activity sheet set to use with the students and explain how to use it.

    - The Plan and Manage Activity Sheets (pages 161–165) are meant for any student who is having difficulty getting started with the project or who is feeling overwhelmed with managing it. Give the student the Brainstorming sheet, Finalizing sheet, and Generating Steps sheet. Give the student one copy of the Step sheet for each step they generate for their project. Instruct them to fill out and work on the Step sheets one at a time. After the student completes the first step, they start on the second step, and so forth, until they have completed all the steps. Then they move on to the Final Product sheet.

- The Project Planner Template, Project Planning Grid, and Project Planner activity sheets (pages 166–168) are meant for students who are a bit more self-directed. These sheets are interchangeable; they use different formats to help students to contemplate the tasks, steps, and materials they need to finish the project. Let each student choose the activity sheet they like best.

- The Planning Deck (pages 169–170) is a simpler planning tool that you can use with younger students. First, print as many copies as you need for your students, then cut apart the cards. For each student, use one cover card and one end card, then fill in with as many step cards as are needed. Remember to consider students' ages, attention spans, and independent work experience. Begin with one to three step cards for young students. You can use more step cards for older students. As a student completes a card, move it to the back of the deck.

2. Model each tool with a completed example and guide students through the first few steps.

3. Check in regularly with students and review their work.

4. At the end of the project, ask your students how well the planning tools worked for them.

Plan and Manage Activity Sheets
BRAINSTORMING

Name _____ **Date** _____

Brainstorm a list of ideas for your project: _____

_____

_____

Share your ideas with two people and get their feedback. What suggestions did they

give you? _____

_____

_____

Narrow your brainstormed list to two ideas. What are they?

_____

_____

Think about these two ideas and how you could accomplish them. _____

_____

_____

Help Anxious Kids in a Stressful World © David Campos and Kathleen McConnell Fad—Free Spirit Publishing

Plan and Manage Activity Sheets
FINALIZING

Name _____ **Date** _____

Of your two favorite brainstormed ideas, which one do you want to work on?

_____

Why did you choose this idea for your final project? _____

_____

_____

Share the topic of your final project with one person. Explain what you plan to do and

how you plan to do it. What suggestions do they have for you? _____

_____

_____

_____

_____

The project due date: _____

Help Anxious Kids in a Stressful World © David Campos and Kathleen McConnell Fad—Free Spirit Publishing

Plan and Manage Activity Sheets
GENERATING STEPS

Name _____   **Date** _____

List the steps you will take to prepare for and complete your project. Think about gathering materials and resources, outlining, feedback, working on a draft, feedback, and finalizing the product.

_____

_____

_____

_____

_____

How many steps are there? _____

Who can help you at each step? _____

_____

_____

Get a Step sheet for each step.

Plan and Manage Activity Sheets
STEP

Name _____ **Date** _____

This is step number _____

Describe the action at this step: _____

_____

_____

_____

What materials or resources do you need for this step? _____

_____

_____

Who can help you with this step? _____

_____

Due date: _____

Help Anxious Kids in a Stressful World © David Campos and Kathleen McConnell Fad—Free Spirit Publishing

Plan and Manage Activity Sheets
FINAL PRODUCT

Name _____ **Date** _____

Turn-in checklist:

❏ I followed directions as I created my project.

❏ I followed the steps I listed.

❏ I met the requirements.

❏ My project has focus and purpose.

❏ My project shows original thought.

❏ I checked my project carefully one last time and fixed any mistakes.

❏ I asked a peer to look at my project and give me feedback to improve it.

❏ My text is clearly written with few or no errors.

❏ I used fonts, colors, graphics, or special effects to enhance the project.

❏ _____

❏ _____

❏ _____

❏ _____

❏ _____

Project Planner Template

Name _____ **Date** _____

Project assignment:	Due date:

Brainstorm ideas:

Final project idea:

Supplies needed to complete the project:

Action plan (steps to complete the project):

Project Planning Grid

Name _____ **Date** _____

Step	What to Do	When It's Due	Materials Needed	Check When Done
1				
2				
3				
4				
5				

Help Anxious Kids in a Stressful World © David Campos and Kathleen McConnell Fad—Free Spirit Publishing

Project Planner

Name _____ **Date** _____

Project description:	Final due date:
Step 1:	Due date:
Step 2:	Due date:
Step 3:	Due date:
Step 4:	Due date:
Step 5:	Due date:

Planning Deck

COVER CARD

The final product: _____

_____

Did you finish? _____

Resources you used: _____

_____

_____

_____

STEP CARD

Step: _____

Due date: _____

What you need and who can help:

_____

_____

_____

_____

STEP CARD

Step: _____

Due date: _____

What you need and who can help:

_____

_____

_____

_____

STEP CARD

Step: _____

Due date: _____

What you need and who can help:

_____

_____

_____

_____

Help Anxious Kids in a Stressful World © David Campos and Kathleen McConnell Fad—Free Spirit Publishing

CONTINUED ➡

Planning Deck *(Continued)*

STEP CARD

Step: _____

Due date: _____

What you need and who can help:

_____

_____

_____

_____

_____

STEP CARD

Step: _____

Due date: _____

What you need and who can help:

_____

_____

_____

_____

_____

STEP CARD

Step: _____

Due date: _____

What you need and who can help:

_____

_____

_____

_____

END CARD

Finished!

What strategies helped you

complete the project?_____

_____

_____

What will you do next time you

have a project to complete?

_____

Help Anxious Kids in a Stressful World © David Campos and Kathleen McConnell Fad—Free Spirit Publishing

ACTION STRATEGY 25

Secret Signals

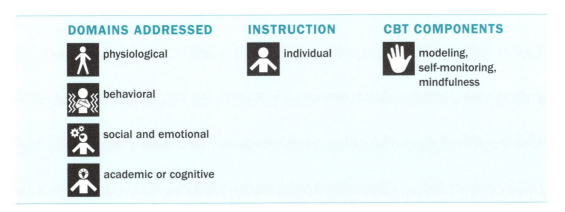

DOMAINS ADDRESSED	INSTRUCTION	CBT COMPONENTS
physiological	individual	modeling, self-monitoring, mindfulness
behavioral		
social and emotional		
academic or cognitive		

Ready

All the action strategies in this book are intended to help students manage anxiety. But how can teachers direct or allow students to use the anxiety-reducing strategies they have learned without embarrassing or calling attention to the students? One simple way is to use a secret signal.

Set

Signals between you and your students can go both ways: students can signal you when they are feeling anxious, overwhelmed, upset, or unable to function well in class. Likewise, you can read the warning signs of anxiety in your students. Maybe they have become quiet and withdrawn; perhaps they are restless and having trouble getting started on an assignment; or maybe they are crying, trembling, and expressing worry. For this strategy, you and a student agree on some signals and then use them when you feel they are necessary.

Go

1. With the student, choose one or two signals and decide what they will mean. They should be nonverbal and not easily interpreted by others, to protect the student's privacy. Some students might be embarrassed by or might not welcome attention from others. Consider using one or two of these examples:

■ **Student Signals**

  ❑ Raise two fingers, making the peace sign.

  ❑ Point to a special sign, image, or picture taped to your desk or the front of your notebook, such as an animal, cartoon character, or celebrity.

  ❑ Hold up a red pencil kept handy just for this purpose.

  ❑ Do one quick finger snap.

  ❑ Raise your index finger.

  ❑ Use a signal card that's on your desk.

  ❑ Put your elbows on your desk and cradle your chin with both hands.

  ❑ Place a red shape on the corner of your desk.

  ❑ Take out your journal and hold it up for a few moments so the teacher can see it.

■ **Teacher Signals**

  ❑ Stop by the student's desk and lightly tap their shoulder.

  ❑ Hum a simple tune that the student knows.

  ❑ Show the ASL sign for help.

  ❑ Tug on your ear.

  ❑ Make eye contact with the student and nod your head.

  ❑ Put your hands together and intertwine your fingers.

  ❑ Stand near the student and lightly knock on their desk.

2. A signal should prompt you or the student to do something, so it is important to establish what response is expected from the signal. It's best to link a single response to a specific signal, as in the following examples. Teach the response to the signal and practice with the student before using it.

  ■ When you point at the clock, the student knows they should move to a quiet area, set a timer for three minutes, and work on a puzzle, read a book, or draw until the timer goes off.

  ■ When the student holds up their journal and you nod, the student knows to write in their journal for three to five minutes.

  ■ When the student puts their hand on their forehead and the teacher mouths the word *yes*, the student can leave to get a drink of water.

3. After using a signal and response, check in with the student when you have an opportunity. Find out how they are feeling, discuss whether the secret signal worked, and make changes if necessary. As you debrief, consider these key questions:

  ■ Did you/I use the signal soon enough to help you avoid serious agitation or anxiety?

  ■ Did you/I respond to the signal soon enough to help you avoid a major problem?

- Did you feel comfortable stopping your work to use a calming strategy?

- Did the strategy that you used work? Afterward, did you feel less anxious?

- What changes could we make to our secret signal system?

- What could you do *before* needing to use a secret signal? How can I help you?

References

American Psychiatric Association. 2013. *Diagnostic and Statistical Manual of Mental Disorders, Fifth Edition* (DSM-5). doi.org/10.1176/appi. books.9780890425596.

Bear, Mark, Barry Connors, and Michael Paradiso. 2020. *Neuroscience: Exploring the Brain, Enhanced Fourth Edition.* Burlington, MA: Jones & Bartlett Learning.

Beesdo, Katja, Susanne Knappe, and Daniel S. Pine. 2009. "Anxiety and Anxiety Disorders in Children and Adolescents: Developmental Issues and Implications for DSM-V." *Psychiatric Clinics of North America* 32 (3): 483–524. doi.org/10.1016/j.psc.2009.06.002.

Bhatia, Manjeet Singh, and Aparna Goyal. 2018. "Anxiety Disorders in Children and Adolescents: Need for Early Detection." *Journal of Postgraduate Medicine* 64 (2): 75–76. doi.org/10.4103/jpgm.JPGM_65_18.

Bitsko, Rebecca H., Joseph R. Holbrook, Reem M. Ghandour, Stephen J. Blumberg, Susanna N. Visser, Ruth Perou, and John T. Walkup. 2018. "Epidemiology and Impact of Health Care Provider–Diagnosed Anxiety and Depression Among US Children." *Journal of Developmental and Behavioral Pediatrics* 39 (5): 395–403. doi.org/10.1097/DBP.0000000000000571.

Bower, Bruce. 2016. "Kids' Anxieties, Depression Need Attention." *Science News.* sciencenews.org/article/kids-anxieties-depression-need-attention.

Burke, Maribeth. 2007. A *Study of Child Anxiety Disorders and Their Impact on the Development of Anxiety Disorders in Adulthood.* Providence College Social Work Theses. digitalcommons.providence.edu/cgi/viewcontent.cgi?article=1002&context=socialwrk_students.

Caldwell, Deborah M., Sarah R. Davies, Sarah E. Hetrick, Jennifer C. Palmer, Paolo Caro, José A. López-López, David Gunnell, Judi Kidger, James Thomas, Clare French, Emily Stockings, Rona Campbell, and Nicky J. Welton. 2019. "School-Based Interventions to Prevent Anxiety and Depression in Children and Young People: A Systematic Review and Network Meta-analysis." *Lancet Psychiatry* 6 (12): 1011–1020. doi.org/10.1016/ 215-0366(19)30403-1.

Challenge Success. 2021. *Kids Under Pressure.* challengesuccess.org/wp-content/uploads/2021/02/CS-NBC-Study-Kids-Under-Pressure-PUBLISHED.pdf.

Chavira, Denise A., Ann Garland, May Yeh, Kristen McCabe, and Richard L. Hough. 2009. "Child Anxiety Disorders and Service Utilization in Public Systems of Care: Comorbidity and Service Utilization." *Journal of Behavioral Health Services & Research* 36 (4): 492–504. doi.org/10.1007/ 1414-008-9139-x.

Child Mind Institute. 2018. "Understanding Anxiety in Children and Teens: 2018 Children's Mental Health Report." childmind.org/awareness-campaigns/childrens-mental-health-report/2018-childrens-mental-health-report.

CASEL. 2022. "Fundamentals of SEL." casel.org/fundamentals-of-sel.

Dias, Valadão F., Juliana Álvares Duarte Bonini Campos, Raquel V. Oliviera, Rosário Mendes, Isabel Leal, and Joao Maroco. 2016. "Causal Factors of Anxiety Symptoms in Children." *Clinical and Experimental Psychology* 2 (2): 1–11. doi.org/10.4172/2471-2701.1000131.

Digitale, Erin. 2021. "Stanford Study Finds Stronger One-Way Fear Signals in Brains of Anxious Kids." *Stanford Medicine News Center.* med.stanford.edu/news/all-news/2020/04/stanford-study-finds-stronger-one-way-fear-signals-in-brains-of-.html.

Dingman, Marc. 2019. *Your Brain, Explained: What Neuroscience Reveals About Your Brain and Its Quirks.* Boston: Nicholas Brealey Publishing.

Donovan, Caroline L., and Sonja March. 2014. "Online CBT for Preschool Anxiety Disorders: A Randomised Control Trial." *Behaviour Research and Therapy* 58: 24–35. doi.org/10.1016/j.brat.2014.05.001.

Durlak, Joseph A., Roger P. Weissberg, Allison B. Dymnicki, Rebecca D. Taylor, and Kriston B. Schellinger. 2011. "The Impact of Enhancing Students' Social and Emotional Learning: A Meta-Analysis of School-Based Universal Interventions." *Child Development* 82 (1): 405–432. doi.org/10.1111/j.1467-8624.2010.01564.x.

Eagleman, David. 2017. *The Brain: The Story of You.* New York: Vintage Books.

Fortin, Jacey, and Giulia Heyward. 2022. "'It's Just Stressful': Students Feel the Weight of Pandemic Uncertainty." *New York Times,* January 30, 2022. nytimes.com/2022/01/30/us/students-pandemic-virtual-learning.html.

Garrett, Bob, and Gerald Hough. 2022. *Brain & Behavior: An Introduction to Behavioral Neuroscience, Sixth Edition.* Thousand Oaks, CA: Sage Publications.

Ginsburg, Golda S., Jeffrey E. Pella, Kate Pisselli, and Grace Chan. 2019. "Teacher Anxiety Program for Elementary Students (TAPES): Intervention Development and Proposed Randomized Controlled Trial." *Trials* 20 (1): 792. doi.org/10.1186/s13063-019-3863-9.

Greenwood, Hayley. 2017. "What It Feels Like to Have Anxiety, Because It Isn't Us 'Being Crazy.'" *Thought Catalog.* thoughtcatalog.com/hayley-greenwood/2017/02/what-it-feels-like-to-have-anxiety-because-it-isnt-us-being-crazy.

Harvard Health Publishing. 2020. "Understanding the Stress Response." *Harvard Health Publishing.* health.harvard.edu/staying-healthy/understanding-the-stress-response.

Herzig-Anderson, Kathleen, Daniela Colognori, Jeremy K. Fox, Catherine E. Stewart, and Carrie Masia Warner. 2012. "School-based Anxiety Treatments for Children and Adolescents." *Child and Adolescent Psychiatry North America* 21 (3): 655–668. doi.org/10.1016/j.chc.2012.05.006.

Hugh-Jones, Siobhan, Sophie Beckett, Ella Tumelty, and Pavan Mallikarjun. 2020. "Indicated Prevention Interventions for Anxiety in Children and Adolescents: A Review and Meta-Analysis of School-Based Programs." *European Child and Adolescent Psychiatry* 30 (6): 849–860. doi.org/10.1007/s00787-020-01564-x.

Hurrell, Katherine E., Jennifer L. Hudson, and Carolyn A. Schniering. 2015. "Parental Reactions to Children's Negative Emotions: Relationships with Emotion Regulation in Children with an Anxiety Disorder." *Journal of Anxiety Disorders* 29: 72–82. doi.org/10.1016/j.janxdis.2014.10.008.

In-Albon, Tina, and Silvia Schneider. 2007. "Psychotherapy of Childhood Anxiety Disorders: A Meta-Analysis." *Psychotherapy and Psychosomatics* 76: 15–24. doi.org/10.1159/000096361.

Jennings, Patricia A., and Mark T. Greenberg. 2009. "The Prosocial Classroom: Teacher Social and Emotional Competence in Relation to Student and Classroom Outcomes." *Review of Educational Research* 79 (1): 491–525. doi.org/10.3102/0034654308325693.

Killu, Kim, and R. Marc A. Crundwell. 2016. "Students with Anxiety in the Classroom: Educational Accommodations and Interventions." *Beyond Behavior* 25 (2): 30–40. doi.org/10.1177/107429561602500205.

Lee, Susanne S., Andrea M. Victor, Matthew G. James, Lauren E. Roach, and Gail A. Bernstein. 2016. "School-Based Interventions for Anxious Children: Long-Term Follow-Up." *Child Psychiatry & Human Development* 47 (2): 183–193. doi.org/10.1007/ 0578-015-0555-x.

McCarthy, Claire. 2019. "Anxiety in Teens Is Rising: What's Going On?" HealthyChildren.org, American Academy of Pediatrics. healthychildren.org/English/health-issues/conditions/emotional-problems/Pages/Anxiety-Disorders.aspx.

McLoone, Jordana, Jennifer L. Hudson, and Ronald M. Rapee. 2006. "Treating Anxiety Disorders in a School Setting." *Education and Treatment of Children* 29 (2): 219–242. jstor.org/stable/42899883.

Medina, John. 2014. *Brain Rules: 12 Principles for Surviving and Thriving at Work, Home, and School, Second Edition.* Seattle: Pear Press.

Minahan, Jessica. 2019. "Tackling Negative Thinking in the Classroom." *Phi Delta Kappan* 101 (3): 26–31. kappanonline.org/tackling-students-negative-thinking-classroom-anxiety-stress-minahan/.

National Center for School Mental Health. 2020. *School Mental Health Quality Guide: Screening.* schoolmentalhealth.org/media/SOM/Microsites/NCSMH/Documents/Quality-Guides/Screening-1.27.20.pdf.

National Scientific Council on the Developing Child. 2010. *Persistent Fear and Anxiety Can Affect Young Children's Learning and Development: Working Paper No. 9.* developingchild.harvard.edu/resources/persistent-fear-and-anxiety-can-affect-young-childrens-learning-and-development.

Oberle, Eva, and Kimberly A. Schonert-Reichl. 2016. "Stress Contagion in the Classroom? The Link Between Classroom Teacher Burnout and Morning Cortisol in Elementary School Students." *Social Science Medicine* 159: 30–37. doi.org/10.1016/j.socscimed.2016.04.031.

Office of the Surgeon General. 2021. "Protecting Youth Mental Health: The U.S. Surgeon General's Advisory." hhs.gov/sites/default/files/surgeon-general-youth-mental-health-advisory.pdf.

Panayiotou, Margarita, Neil Humphrey, and Michael Wigelsworth. 2019. "An Empirical Basis for Linking Social and Emotional Learning to Academic Performance." *Contemporary Educational Psychology* 56: 193–204. doi.org/10.1016/j.cedpsych.2019.01.009.

Pew Research Center. 2015. "The American Family Today." pewresearch.org/social-trends/ 2015/12/17/1-the-american-family-today.

Racine, Nicole, Brae Anne McArthur, and Jessica E. Cooke. 2021. "Global Prevalence of Depressive and Anxiety Symptoms in Children and Adolescents During COVID-19." *JAMA Pediatrics* 175 (11): 1142–1150. doi.org/10.1001/jamapediatrics.2021.2482.

Rapee, Ronald M. 2018. "Anxiety Disorders in Children and Adolescents: Nature, Development, Treatment and Prevention." In *IACAPAP e-Textbook of Child and Adolescent Mental Health,* edited by Joseph M. Rey. Geneva: International Association for Child and Adolescent Psychiatry and Allied Professions. iacapap.org/_Resources/Persistent/dcdfa875541149469ff8dda50fe3c5c249bb 99c8/F.1-Anxiety-Disorders-2018-UPDATE.pdf.

Reynolds, Katharine C., and Candice A. Alfano. 2016. "Things That Go Bump in the Night: Frequency and Predictors of Nightmares in Anxious and Non-anxious Children." *Behavioral Sleep Medicine* 14 (4): 442–456. ncbi.nlm.nih.gov/pmc/articles/PMC7388348.

Science News, eds. 1966. "50 Years Ago: Childhood Fears Are Common, Normal." *Science News* 189 (13): 4. sciencenews.org/archive/childhood-fears-are-common-normal.

Schaefer, Charles E., and Athena A. Drewes. 2018. "Play-Based Approaches for Treating Childhood Anxieties: Basic Concepts and Practices." In *Play-Based Interventions for Childhood Anxiety, Fears, and Phobias,* edited by Athena A. Drewes and Charles E. Schafer, 3–12. New York: Guilford Press.

Schwartz, Christine, Jenny Lou Barican, Donna Yung, Yufei Zheng, and Charlotte Waddell. 2019. "Six Decades of Preventing and Treating Childhood Anxiety Disorders: A Systematic Review and Meta-Analysis to Inform Policy and Practice." *Evidence-Based Mental Health* 22 (3): 103–110. doi.org/10.1136/ebmental-2019-300096.

US Department of Education, Office of Special Education and Rehabilitative Services. 2021. *Supporting Child and Student Social, Emotional, Behavioral, and Mental Health Needs.* ed.gov/documents/students/supporting-child-student-social-emotional-behavioral-mental-health.pdf.

Vallance, Aaron K., and Victoria Fernandez. 2016. "Anxiety Disorders in Children and Adolescents: Aetiology, Diagnosis and Treatment." *BJPsych Advances* 22 (5): 335–344. doi.org/10.1192/apt.bp.114.014183.

Wehry, Anna M., Katja Beesdo-Baum, Meghann M. Hennelly, Sucheta D. Connolly, and Jeffrey R. Strawn. 2015. "Assessment and Treatment of Anxiety Disorders in Children and Adolescents." *Current Psychiatry Reports* 17 (7): 52. doi.org/10.1007/ 1920-015-0591-z.

Weir, Kirsten. 2017. "Brighter Futures for Anxious Kids." *Monitor on Psychology* 48 (3): 50. apa.org/monitor/2017/03/anxious-kids.

Werner-Seidler, Aliza, Yael Perry, Alison L. Calear, Jill M. Newby, and Helen Christensen. 2017. "School-Based Depression and Anxiety Prevention Programs for Young People: A Systematic Review and Meta-analysis." *Clinical Psychology Review* 51: 30–47. doi.org/10.1016/j.cpr.2016.10.005.

Yale Medicine. 2023. "Childhood Stress and Anxiety." *Yale Medicine.* yalemedicine.org/conditions/childhood-stress-and-anxiety.

Ybañez-Llorente, Kathy. 2014. "Addressing Anxiety in School Settings: Information for Counselors." ACA Knowledge Center. counseling.org/docs/default-source/vistas/article_62.pdf?sfvrsn=20677d2c_10.

Index

action strategies involving components of, 57

favorable outcomes of, 43

goals of, 43–44

limited availability of, 44

schools using components of, 44–45. *See also* specific components

Cognitive challenges, 28–29

Cognitive distortions, 18. *See also* Negative thoughts/thinking patterns

Cognitive restructuring (CBT component), 44, 45

action strategies using, 73–77, 88–91, 92–96, 106–107, 108–110, 111–114, 129–132, 133–135, 143–145

Collaborative for Academic, Social, and Emotional Learning (CASEL), 47

Concentration, lack of, 55

Conditioning, 37–38

Cool Kids Anxiety Program, 46

Cool Little Kids Plus Social Skills, 46

Coping and Promoting Strength, 46

Coping Toolbox, 56, 59, 119–120

Counseling, 43

COVID-19 pandemic, 1, 3–6, 48

Cue cards

Calm-Down, 116, 118

Countdown, 84, 86–87

Deep Breathing, 81–82

I Need a Friend, 122, 125

Visual Cue Cards, 143–145

Yet! and Right Now!, 134, 135

D

Deep Breathing Exercises, 56, 58, 78–82

Depression, 4, 25

De-Stress Your Directions, 56, 60, 150–152

Diagnosed anxiety disorders. *See* Anxiety disorders

Diagnostic and Statistical Manual of Mental Disorders, Fifth Edition (DSM-5), 2, 19–20

Diagnostic frameworks, 2

Directions, giving, 150–152

Divorce, parental, 26

Downward spirals, 28–30

Drawing activities, 66, 71, 75, 90, 91, 93, 129, 130, 154

Drills, school, 34

Drug use/addiction, 26

DSM. See Diagnostic and Statistical Manual of Mental Disorders, Fifth Edition (DSM-5)

Dysfunction, household, 26

E

Echo strategy, for giving directions, 152

Education, diagnostic framework for anxiety in, 2

Emotional abuse, 26

Emotional regulation, 19, 36, 39

Emotional symptoms, 28

Emotions, action strategy to help students understand and identify their, 139–142

Environmental causes of anxiety, 33

Even/Odd Partners question-and-answer structure, 136–138

Everyone Move!, 56, 59

Excessive worry, 55

about public embarrassment, 136

instructional structures designed to prevent, 136–138

My Worry Plan for, 88–91

over school assignments, planning tools for, 159–170

Executive functioning, 35, 55

Exercise(s). *See* Physical exercise(s), action strategies involving

Exposure (CBT component)

about, 44

action strategies using, 136–138, 150–152, 153–158, 159–170

F

Fear(s)

across the lifespan, 25–26, 74

anxiety *versus*, 18

becoming conditioned, 37–38

typical, 9 months-adulthood, 16

Fernandez, Victoria, 17

Fight, flight, freeze, or fawn response, 35, 49, 53

Five Minutes, Five Movements activity, 109–110

Focus Cards, 97–98, 102–105

Fortune-telling, 74, 133

4-4-4 Breathing, 79, 81

Friendly Countdown, 85, 87

Friends/friendships, 20, 29, 121–125

Full-Body Rock, Papers, Scissors, 110

G

Gender, prevalence of anxiety and, 24

Generalized anxiety disorder, 20, 21, 24, 26, 43

Genetic causes of anxiety, 32

Go, Move, Focus, 56, 58, 97–105

Gratitude and Gratitude Journal, 56, 59, 92–96, 129–132

Greenwood, Hayley, 29

H

Hippocampus, 35

Hypothalamus, 35, 36

I

IEPs (individualized education programs), 2, 8, 15, 43, 62

Images, uplifting and positive, 106–107

Individuals with Disabilities Education Act (IDEA), 2

Infancy, anxiety present in human, 16, 25

Interventions, 14–15. *See also* School-based interventions

In the Research, 10, 15, 26, 30, 36, 43

J

Journal(ing), 64, 66, 129–132

K

Kiss Breathing, 79, 82

L

Learned helplessness, 29

Loneliness, childhood, 1, 28

Lonely Kids in a Connected World: What Teachers Can Do, 1

Look, Listen, Feel Cards, 97–98, 99–101

M

Maladaptive anxiety, 16, 17

Maladaptive thinking patterns, 38

Medical condition, anxiety disorder due to, 20

Medical diagnosis of anxiety, 2

Medication(s), 24, 43, 44, 61

Medication-induced anxiety disorder, 20

Medina, John, 35

Memory impairment, 55

Mental health and mental health conditions

addressed through school-based programs, 46–47

social and emotional learning (SEL) and, 47, 52

students with anxiety having additional, 53

teachers' role in helping students deal with, 6–7, 15

academic or cognitive, 5, 28, 55

behavioral, 27, 53–54

generalized anxiety disorder, 21

physiological, 27, 53

recognizing, 68–72

social and emotional, 28, 54

Silly voices, repeating directions in, 152

Skills for Academic and Social Success, 46

Social and emotional domain/issues, 28, 42, 54

    action strategies addressing, 56, 58–60, 63–67, 68–72, 73–77, 78–82, 88–91, 92–96, 106–107, 108–110, 111–114, 115–118, 119–120, 121–125, 126–128, 129–132, 133–135, 136–138, 150–152, 171–173

Social and emotional learning (SEL), 47–48, 52

Social anxiety (disorder), 19, 20–21, 24, 26, 43

    Working in Twos action strategy to prevent, 136–138

Social awareness (SEL competency), 48

Social downward spiral, 29–30

Social isolation, 30, 54, 55

Social media, 6, 34

Social skills, 20–21, 29–30. *See also* Social and emotional domain/issues

Song-and-Dance Countdown, 84, 86

Special needs children, 1

SSRIs (selective serotonin reuptake inhibitors), 43

Step-by-Step Project Planners, 56, 60, 159–170

Stranger anxiety, 25

Stress

    behaviors related to, 5

    classroom practices to reduce, 35

    COVID-19 pandemic and, 3

    De-Stress Your Directions action strategy addressing, 150–152

    teachers experiencing, 48

Stress balls, 117

Stress contagion, 48

Stress response system, 35–37

Strongest Families Institute, 46

Students of color, prevalence of stress among, 3

Students with anxiety. *See also* Childhood anxiety

    behaviors in school, 7–8, 17

    with diagnosed anxiety disorders, 14–15

downward spirals of, 28–30

information-processing errors by, 38–39

signals to teachers given by, 172

statements by, during COVID-19 pandemic, 3–4

that are not diagnosed with anxiety disorders, 14

Substance-induced anxiety disorder, 20

T

Teachers

    anxiety interventions by, 46–47

    being equipped to intervene with students' anxiety, 15

    directions given by, 150–152

    impact on child's mental health and emotional well-being, 6–7

    self-care strategies for, 48

    signals to students given by, 172

    staying attuned and checking in with students, 24

A Team of Friends, 56, 59, 121–125

Temperamental causes of anxiety, 33

Thankfulness, 92–96, 111–114, 129–132

Thanks for Three, 56, 58, 92–96

Therapy, 7, 24, 44. *See also* Cognitive behavioral therapy (CBT)

Threat beliefs, 38

Timid to Tiger (anxiety program), 46

Toddlers, anxiety in, 25

Track Anxiety Using a Calendar, 56, 58, 63–67

Treatment, 24. *See also* Cognitive behavioral therapy (CBT); School-based interventions

V

Vallance, Aaron, 17

Videos, 154

Violence, 3, 26

Visual Cue Cards, 56, 60, 143–145

Visual cues, when giving directions, 150

Visualization (CBT component)

    about, 45

    action strategies using, 83–87, 106–107, 115–118

Visualization Countdown, 56, 58, 83–87

Visual Scheduling, 56, 60, 146–149

Visual supports

    images triggering positive feelings, 106–107

to relieve anxiety when anticipating situations, 154

used when giving directions, 150

Visual Cue Cards, 143–145

W

Walking, action strategy involving, 97–105

What Not to Think, 56, 58, 73–77

Working in Twos, 56, 59, 136–138

Worry, 16, 18. *See also* Anxiety; Excessive worry

    about parents'/caregivers' welfare, 20

    Box of Worries action strategy for, 126–128

    worry-based thinking, 83

Writing activities, 91. *See also* Journal(ing)

    about positive thinking or thankfulness, 93

    about upcoming lessons and assignments, 154

    Box of Worries, 127–129

    Gratitude Journal, 129–132

    for My Worry Plan, 88, 91

    for tracking anxiety, 64

    for What to Think Instead action strategy, 75

Y

Yet and Right Now, 56, 59, 133–135

Young adults, 26

Digital Resources

A fillable PDF of each teacher reflection form and student activity sheet is available on TCM Content Cloud.

Accessing the Digital Resources

The digital resources can be downloaded by following these steps:

1. Go to www.tcmpub.com/digital

2. Use the 13-digit ISBN number to redeem the digital resources.

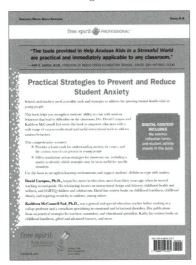

3. Respond to the question using the book.

4. Follow the prompts on the Content Cloud website to sign in or create a new account.

5. The content redeemed will appear on your My Content screen. Click on the product to look through the digital resources. All file resources are available for download. Select files can be previewed, opened, and shared. Any web-based content, such as videos, links, or interactive text, can be viewed and used in the browser but is not available for download.

For questions and assistance with your ISBN redemption, please contact Teacher Created Materials.

email: customerservice@tcmpub.com

phone: 800-858-7339

About the Authors

David Campos began his career in education more than thirty years ago, when he started teaching second grade. He earned his Ph.D. from The University of Texas at Austin, specializing in learning disabilities and behavior disorders. His scholarship focuses on instructional design and delivery, childhood health and wellness, and LGBTQ children and adolescents. He has written books on childhood loneliness, childhood obesity, and inspiring creativity in students, among others. He lives in San Antonio, Texas.

Kathleen McConnell Fad has a Ph.D. in learning disabilities and behavior disorders from The University of Texas at Austin. Kathy was a general and special education teacher before working as a college professor and a consultant specializing in emotional and behavioral disorders. Her publications focus on practical strategies for teachers, counselors, and educational specialists. Kathy has written books on childhood loneliness, gifted and advanced learners, and more. She lives in Austin, Texas.